DR. ACKERMAN'S BOOK OF THE
ROTTWEILER

LOWELL ACKERMAN DVM

BB-101

Overleaf: Redhill's Duke Ruger of Arden, CGC, owned by Kelly M. Skiptunas.

The author has exerted every effort to ensure that medical information mentioned in this book is in accord with current recommendations and practice at the time of publication. However, in view of the ongoing advances in veterinary medicine, the reader is urged to consult with a veterinarian regarding individual health issues.

Photographers: Christine Filler, Isabelle Francais, Jeff Greene, Judith P. Iby, Ray Matty, Barb McNinch, Ron Reagen, Shamraach Rottweilers, Kelly M. Skiptunas.

The presentation of pet products in this book is strictly for instructive purposes only; it does not constitute an endorsement by the author, publisher, owners of dogs portrayed, or any other contributors.

© 1996 by LOWELL ACKERMAN DVM

Distributed in the UNITED STATES to the Pet Trade by T.F.H. Publications, Inc., One T.F.H. Plaza, Neptune City, NJ 07753; distributed in the UNITED STATES to the Bookstore and Library Trade by National Book Network, Inc. 4720 Boston Way, Lanham MD 20706; in CANADA to the Pet Trade by H & L Pet Supplies Inc., 27 Kingston Crescent, Kitchener, Ontario N2B 2T6; Rolf C. Hagen Inc., 3225 Sartelon St. Laurent-Montreal Quebec H4R 1E8; in CANADA to the Book Trade by Vanwell Publishing Ltd., 1 Northrup Crescent, St. Catharines, Ontario L2M 6P5 ; in ENGLAND by T.F.H. Publications, PO Box 15, Waterlooville PO7 6BQ; in AUSTRALIA AND THE SOUTH PACIFIC by T.F.H. (Australia), Pty. Ltd., Box 149, Brookvale 2100 N.S.W., Australia; in NEW ZEALAND by Brooklands Aquarium Ltd. 5 McGiven Drive, New Plymouth, RD1 New Zealand; in Japan by T.F.H. Publications, Japan—Jiro Tsuda, 10-12-3 Ohjidai, Sakura, Chiba 285, Japan; in SOUTH AFRICA by Lopis (Pty) Ltd., P.O. Box 39127, Booysens, 2016, Johannesburg, South Africa. Published by T.F.H. Publications, Inc.

MANUFACTURED IN THE
UNITED STATES OF AMERICA
BY T.F.H. PUBLICATIONS, INC.

CONTENTS

DEDICATION

To my wonderful wife Susan and my three adorable children, Nadia, Rebecca and David.

PREFACE

Keeping your Rottweiler healthy is the most important job that you, as an owner, can do. Whereas there are many books available that deal with breed qualities, conformation and show characteristics, this may be the only book available dedicated entirely to the preventative health care of the Rottweiler. This information has been compiled from a variety of sources and assembled here to provide you with the most up-to-date advice available.

This book will take you through the important stages of selecting your pet, screening it for inherited medical and behavioral problems, meeting its nutritional needs, and seeing that it receives optimal medical care.

So, enjoy the book and use the information to keep your Rottweiler the healthiest it can be for a long, full and rich life.

Lowell Ackerman DVM

BIOGRAPHY

D r. Lowell Ackerman is a world-renowned veterinary clinician, author, lecturer and radio personality. He is a Diplomate of the American College of Veterinary Dermatology and is a consultant in the fields of dermatology, nutrition and genetics. Dr. Ackerman is the author of 34 books and over 150 book chapters and articles. He also hosts a national radio show on pet health care and moderates a site on the World Wide Web dedicated to pet health care issues (**http://www.familyinternet.com/pet/pet-vet.htm**).

BREED HISTORY

**THE GENESIS OF THE
MODERN ROTTWEILER**

The exact genealogy of the Rottweiler is lost in antiquity, but it is supposed that the breed originally descended from Roman drover dogs over a thousand years ago. The town name of Rottweil is derived from an ex-cavation of a Roman bath on that location (from *Rote Wil*, red tile). There were many

Facing page: Likely of Roman drover dog descent, the Rottweiler was very valuable to Roman cattlemen over a thousand years ago.

cattlemen and butchers in the town of Rottweil in mediaeval times and the descendants of those Roman drover dogs (now Rottweilers) were valuable workers in the cattle trade.

The breed fell on hard times by the middle of the 19th century when their duties were largely replaced by railroads and donkeys. It wasn't until the 20th century that the breed started to make a comeback and gained some popularity as police dogs. The Allgemeiner Deutscher Rottweiler Klub (ADRK) was formed in 1921, and the first official stud book was published in 1924. The first Rottweilers made it to America in time for the great stock market crash of 1929; the first Rottweiler was admitted to the American Kennel Club Stud Book in 1931. In 1994, the Rot-

Rottweilers have a natural herding instinct, which makes them excellent farm dogs. They are capable of herding small and large animals alike.

After a period of neglect, Rottweilers made their comeback as police dogs and guard dogs in the early 20th century and came to America in the late 1920s.

tweiler was the second most commonly registered breed with the American Kennel Club. When you consider how popular the breed is today, it is truly amazing to acknowledge its humble beginnings and meteoric rise over such a short period of time.

MIND & BODY

**PHYSICAL AND BEHAVIORAL TRAITS
OF THE ROTTWEILER**

Confident, calm, and courageous, the Rottweiler defines the guard dog and companion animal. Rottweilers desire to protect their homes and loved ones, taking their roles as guardians most seriously. Most importantly, the Rottweiler is a-

daptable and tractable. Any Rottweiler that proves difficult to

*Facing page:
As the top
guard dog
breed, the
Rottweiler is
adaptable
and tractable.*

control, unfriendly toward his own, and fearful is not a Rottweiler, regardless of his black and tan markings!

CONFORMATION AND PHYSICAL CHARACTERISTICS

This is not a book about show dogs, so information here will not deal with the conformation of champions and how to select one. The purpose of this chapter is to provide basic information about the stature of a Rottweiler and qualities of a physical nature.

Clearly beauty is in the eye of the beholder. Since standards come and standards go, measuring your dog against some imaginary yardstick does little for you or your dog. Just because your dog isn't a show champion doesn't mean that he or she is any less of a family member, and likewise, just because a dog is a champion doesn't mean that he or she is not a genetic time bomb waiting to go off.

When breeders and those interested in showing Rottweilers are selecting dogs, they are looking for those qualities that match the breed "standard." This standard, however, is of an imaginary Rottweiler and it changes from time to time and from country to country. Thus, the conformation and physical character-istics that pet owners should concentrate on are somewhat different and much more practical.

Rottweilers were originally bred to be medium-sized dogs, but as they were used for more and more guard work, they were bred to become progressively larger and more robust. Most adult males are 24-27 inches (61-68 cm) at the withers, and bitches are about 2 inches (5 cm) smaller. Larger dogs are not necessarily better dogs. Rottweilers were never intended to be considered "giants," and the increased size might promote some medical problems that tend to be more common in larger dogs. There is some preliminary evidence that the larger members of the breed might be more susceptible to orthopedic disorders, such as elbow dysplasia and hip dysplasia.

COAT COLOR, CARE, AND CONDITION

There is only one "approved" color for Rottweilers—black with rust to mahogany markings. The various standards even dictate where the rust to mahogany markings should be present and where they should be absent. This has no associated health implications. Likewise, breeders try to attain a coat that is medium length, straight and coarse. Most consider a wavy or curly coat to be a "fault," even though it has no impact on the health of the animal. Similarly, breeders want an undercoat that doesn't show through the outer coat, and the outer coat itself should be neither too long nor too short.

With all the fuss over coat condition, most owners will not need to worry much about coat care. Rottweilers don't really require regular "trimming," al-though all would benefit from routine brushing. For the Rott-weiler pet, bathing is only needed when the animal gets dirty. A hypoallergenic cleansing shampoo is a good choice since few Rottweilers require medicated products. Al-though a scaly keratinization disorder (seborrhea) has re-cently been reported in the Rottweiler, the breed has a relatively low incidence of skin problems.

Although coat trimming isn't necessary, regular brushing is essential for your Rottweiler. Brushing removes dead skin and hair coat.

As much as Rottweilers love to get wet, bathing your pet Rottweiler is only necessary when he becomes dirty. If you plan to show your Rottweiler, you will need to bathe him more regularly.

PERSONALITY AND BEHAVIOR OF THE ACTIVE ROTTWEILER
by Barbara McNinch

Personality

The personality of the Rottweiler is at once engaging and imposing. Though they are often standoffish at first, they will make friends readily with new people and love to have attention. In fact, once you make friends with a Rottweiler, you have a friend for life. Be prepared to play ball, pet and cuddle!

Rottweilers are fiercely devoted to the members of their families. When raised with love, respect and training, they are loyal and protective of everyone. They are especially fond of children and will follow them everywhere, watching over them zealously. Their herding background makes them ideally suited to keeping track of not only people but things. They will tend to the house and its contents with great supervisory skills!

In the case of threatening or questionable people, the Rottweiler is as intimidating as he is friendly. He is alert to his surroundings and will notice when something is amiss.

The well-tempered animal will inform his owners of intruders, first. However, if no one is home or there is a real threat, he will often independently decide to act protectively.

It is a misnomer that Rottweilers will attack randomly or

that they can't be trusted with children. When bred well and raised from puppyhood with good training and leadership, Rottweilers are fine companions for all members of a household. On average, Rottweilers do not need extra protection training.

The ideal Rottweiler is neither aggressive nor "bossy" but rather a loving family member with good self-esteem and acceptance of position in the family "pack." Because the Rottweiler is a powerful dog and can cause much damage, it is worth spending the time when selecting a pup to pay attention to any evidence of

Devotion to family activities and chores is a top priority for Rottweilers. They understand their position in the family "pack" and know their responsibilities.

In this family carting activity, Shadetree-Stonycreek Liberty, CGC, TDI helps to disclaim the rumor that Rottweilers can't be trusted with children. Owner, Beth Fitzgerald.

personality problems. It is also imperative that all Rottweilers be obedience trained. Like any dog, they have the potential to be vicious without appropriate training. Consider obedience classes mandatory for your sake and that of your dog.

Behavior

There are always certain behaviors that seem inherent within breeds and the Rottweiler is certainly no exception. While it is never wise to stereotype a breed with either good or bad characteristics, there are actually some behaviors that do appear within the breed on a regular basis, regardless of family heritage.

One common trait seen throughout the world of Rottweilers is the grumble. This is a low growling or grumbling coming from deep in the throat of the dog. This usually occurs when the dog is being petted and hugged and is somewhat surprising when first encountered by new owners. The grumbling sound is usually harmless and means simply that the dog is enjoying himself. Conversely, any snapping and biting accompanied by growling or snarling are not acceptable behaviors. The difference in the two is usually separated clearly, with the former occurring only when being stroked or cuddled and minus the lip curling.

Another common love of Rottweilers everywhere is flipping over on the back, all feet in the air. They assume this position for a variety of reasons. One is in conjunction with being rubbed on the belly and is the most common time to hear them grumbling. However, the position is also popular for sleeping and for playing. Rottweiler puppies often sleep with all four feet in the air and propped against a wall or piece of furniture. In addition, when playing with a toy they particularly love, they will flip into the position and literally hold the item between the paws. Thus, they will admire it from a distance, bring it to their mouth to chew a bit, and then once again thrust it out to admire. Anyone who owns a Rottweiler will tell you that this is a common scene in their house.

Activities

It is highly suggested that owners find at least one activity they enjoy doing with their Rottweilers. Since the breed's heritage is that of a worker, having a job to do does a world of good for their attitude and energy level!

Obedience: AKC, UKC and

Settling down for a nap, this Rottweiler assumes the favorite position of the breed. Flipping over on his back with his feet in the air is also great for tummy rubs.

other registries all offer trials and shows at which owners can compete for obedience titles for Rottweilers. There are various levels of difficulty including the Novice, Open and Utility titles. Even novice handlers achieve obedience titles as long as they are willing to do a little work. There is also less demanding fun in the obedience arena via fun matches put on by kennel clubs and obedience clubs. For information on obedience training, contact your veterinarian, local kennel clubs or 4-H extension office.

Agility: This is a great way to exercise your Rottweiler and have lots of fun too. There is also AKC competition within the agility field, enabling participants to earn titles. The agility course consists of a maze of tunnels, jumps, weaving poles, and ramps that the dog must negotiate cleanly and quickly. It is a timed event with the fastest and most accurate dogs winning. Most agility classes require completion of a basic obedience course before enrollment.

Schutzhund: This German sport is a little more time and labor intensive than some, but for the diligent it can be a supremely rewarding activity. Schutzhund consists of three sections, tested and scored individually. The dog must pass each section to earn a title. The titles are gradually harder and are Schutzhund I, II and III. The sections are Obedience, Tracking and Protection. The dog must do a variety of hard work, such as retrieve a 1 to 4 lb. dumbbell

Herding: One of the first jobs the Rottweiler ever had was herding cattle. The breed herds all sizes of animals and often herds children when the instinct is high. Herding is a specialized field of training. When approached from the beginning of the dog's life, it is a highly rewarding job and activity for the dog. It can be difficult to locate trainers, but the sport is becom-

Seemingly a perfect sport for Rottweilers, Schutzhund consists of three sections: obedience, tracking and protection. Owner, Bill Alexander.

over a high wall; find, hold, attack and escort a "prisoner;" and follow a track to its end while finding and indicating objects on the track to his handler. Schutzhund clubs can be hard to find; thoroughly research any clubs you consider, as bad methods can ruin a good dog.

ing more popular among Rottweiler enthusiasts.

Tracking: AKC tracking events are in all areas of the country. This highly enjoyable sport is gaining popularity among Rottweiler owners. The TD (Tracking Dog) and TDX (Tracking Dog Excellent) are the titles available to trackers. There are a number of good books and videos available on teaching the dog to track, and it is one of the few activities often done quite successfully almost virtually on one's own. It is particularly suitable for older dogs who need activity but can no longer do strenuous jumping or running. It is also wonderful light exercise for the dog with dysplastic hips or arthritic conditions.

Making sure that everything is packed, Nancy Thomason's Rottweiler puppy gets ready to go camping.

Carting: Another of the original purposes of the Rottweiler was pulling the cart to market. Rottweiler carting competitions are also lots of fun for the whole family. Besides competitions, carting with the dog can be utilitarian. Many people use their dogs to help them in daily chores around the farm or home. In addition, many Rottweilers are regular parade participants. Carting books and videos are available from many dog magazines and catalogs.

Backpacking/Camping: Fast on the heels of carting, backpacking and camping activities are becoming quite popular with Rottweilers and their families. Many people spend the summer vacation at local state parks enjoying the trails and nature. A well-trained and fit Rottweiler is right at home carrying his own supplies in a specially made backpack. Once again, the working heritage of this breed lends itself to fun and helpfulness.

Whatever activities you choose to participate in with your Rottweiler, make sure you research the training methods, rules of competition and laws that may affect you in your area. Make sure your dog is physically and mentally able to perform the task you have in mind. This includes a thorough checkup including radiographs (x-rays) of the hips and elbows. In addition, make sure you condition the dog for strenuous work gradually and provide proper nutrition and care. Most of all, have fun with your Rottweiler!

SELECTING

**WHAT YOU NEED TO KNOW TO FIND
THE BEST ROTTWEILER PUPPY**

Owning the perfect Rottweiler rarely happens by accident. On the other hand, owning a genetic dud is almost always the result of an impulsive purchase and failure to do even basic research. Buying this book is a major step in understanding the situation and making intelligent choices.

Facing page: When getting a Rottweiler puppy, be certain that genetic screening has been done on the parents. If not, move on.

Don't get caged into buying a Rottweiler that you're not sure about. With so many Rottweilers to choose from, you can afford to be selective. Owner, Pamela Grant.

SOURCES

Recently, a large survey was done to determine whether there were more problems seen in animals adopted from pet stores, breeders, private owners or animal shelters. Somewhat surprisingly, there didn't appear to be any major difference in total number of problems seen from these sources. What was different were the kinds of problems seen in each source. Thus, you can't rely on any one source because there are no standards by which judgments can be made. Most veterinarians will recommend that you select a "good breeder," but there is no way to identify such an individual. A breeder of champion show dogs may also be a breeder of genetic defects.

The best approach is to select a pup from a source that regularly performs genetic screening and has documentation to prove it. If you are intending to be a pet owner, don't worry about whether your pup is show quality. A mark here or there that might disqualify the pup as a show winner has absolutely no impact on its ability to be a loving and healthy pet. Also, the vast majority of dogs will be neutered and not used for breeding anyway. Concentrate on the things that are important.

MEDICAL SCREENING

Whether you are dealing with a breeder, a breed rescue group, a shelter or a pet store, your approach should be the same. You want to identify a Rottweiler that you can live with and screen it for medical and behavioral problems before you make it a permanent family member. If the source you select has not done the important testing needed, make sure they will offer you a health/temperament guarantee before you remove

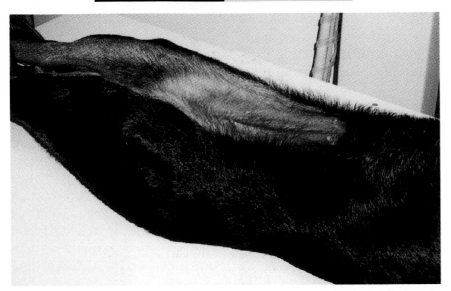

Organizations such as OFA, GDC and Project TEACH™ screen animals for genetic problems. This Rottweiler is being radiographed for hip dysplasia.

the dog from the premises to have the work done yourself. If this is not acceptable, or they are offering an exchange-only policy — keep moving; this isn't the right place for you to get a dog. As soon as you purchase a Rottweiler, pup or adult, go to your veterinarian for a thorough evaluation and testing.

Pedigree analysis is best left to true enthusiasts, but there are some things that you can do even as a novice. Inbreeding is to be discouraged, so check out your four or five generation pedigree and look for names that appear repeatedly. Most breeders linebreed, which is acceptable, so you may see the same

prefix many times but not the same actual dog or bitch. Reputable breeders will usually not allow inbreeding at least three generations back in the puppy's pedigree. Also ask the breeder to provide registration numbers on all ancestors in the pedigree for which testing is done through OFA (Orthopedic Foundation For Animals) and CERF (Canine Eye Registration Foundation). If there are a lot of gaps, the breeder has some explaining to do.

The screening procedure is easier if you select an older dog. Animals can be registered for hips and elbows as young as two years of age by the Orthopedic

Foundation for Animals and by one year of age by Genetic Disease Control (GDC). This is your insurance against hip dysplasia and elbow dysplasia later in life, and both of these conditions are extremely common in the Rottweiler. In addition to the forms of osteochondrosis that affect the elbow joint, Rottweilers are also prone to a form that affects the lower aspects of the hind legs. A verbal testimonial that

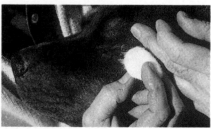

"Clear" eyes requires more than cotton. CERF screens dogs for heritable eye diseases and certifies them as "clear" if none is present. It is best to see your vet regularly in order to be sure your Rottweiler's eyes are free from any problems. Breeder/owner, Ron Gibson.

they've never heard of the condition in their lines is not adequate and probably means they really don't know if they have a problem. Move along.

Evaluation is somewhat more complicated in the Rottweiler puppy. The PennHip™ procedure can determine risk for de-veloping hip dysplasia in pups as young as 16 weeks of age. For pups younger than that, you should request copies of OFA or GDC registration for both parents. If the parents haven't both been registered, their hip and elbow status should be considered unknown and questionable.

For animals older than one year of age, your veterinarian may also want to take a blood sample to check for thyroid function, heartworm status and organ function. This will provide a "baseline" for comparisons as the dog gets older.

Your veterinarian should also perform a very thorough ophthalmologic (eye) examination. The most common eye problems in Rottweilers are cataracts, persistent pupillary membranes, corneal ulcers and retinal dysplasia. It is best to acquire a pup whose parents have both been screened for heritable eye diseases and certified "clear" by organizations such as CERF. If this has been the case, an examination by your veterinarian is probably sufficient and referral to an ophthalmologist is only necessary if recommended by your veterinarian.

BEHAVIORAL SCREENING

Medical screening is important, but don't forget tempera-

Because of their protective nature, Rottweilers can be vicious if not properly trained. Even then, some dogs may have an aggressive temperament disorder, and Schutzhund training for such dogs is highly discouraged.

ment. More dogs are killed each year for behavioral reasons than for all medical problems combined. Temperament testing is a valuable, although not infallible, tool in the screening process. The reason that temperament is so important is that many dogs are eventually destroyed because they exhibit undesirable behaviors. Although not all behaviors are evident in young pups (e.g., aggression often takes many months to manifest itself), detecting anxious and fearful pups (and avoiding them) can be very important in the selection process. Traits most identifiable in the young pup include: fear, ex-

citability, low pain threshold, extreme submission, and noise sensitivity.

Pups can be evaluated for temperament as early as seven to eight weeks of age. Some behaviorists, breeders and trainers recommend objective testing, where scores are given in several different categories. Others are more casual about the process since it is only a crude indicator anyway. In general, the evaluation takes place in three stages by someone the pup has not been exposed to. The testing is not done within 72 hours of vaccination or surgery. First, the pup is observed and handled to determine its sociability. Puppies with obvious undesirable traits such as shyness, overactivity or uncontrollable biting may turn out to be unsuitable. Second, the desired pup is separated from the others and then observed for how it responds when played with and called. Third, the pup should be stimulated in various ways and its responses noted. Suitable activities include: lying the pup on its side, grooming it, clipping its nails, gently grasping it around the muzzle and testing its reactions to noise. In a study conducted at the Psychology Department of Colorado State University, they also found that heart rate was a good indicator in this third stage of evaluation. Actually, they noted the resting heart rate, stimulated the pup with a loud noise, and measured how long it took the heart rate to recover to resting level. Most pups recovered within 36 seconds. Dogs that took considerably longer were more likely to be anxious.

Puppy aptitude tests (PAT) can be given in which a numerical score is given for 11 different traits, with a 1 representing the most assertive or aggressive ex-

Puppy aptitude tests (PATs) help to determine a puppy's sociability. One of the many tests is retrieving, which this Rottweiler pup has down to a science with his Gumabone®.

Rottweilers, if taught when young, can get along with any household pet. Black Forest Tia loves her tiny friend Fitz von Raach.

pression of a trait and a 6 representing disinterest, independence or inaction. The traits assessed in the PAT include: social attraction to people, following, restraint, social dominance, elevation (lifting off ground by evaluator), retrieving, touch sensitivity, sound sensitivity, prey/chase drive, stability, and energy level. Although the tests do not absolutely predict behaviors, they do tend to do well at predicting puppies at behavioral extremes.

ORGANIZATIONS

Project TEACH™ (Training and Education in Animal Care and Health) is a voluntary accreditation process for those individuals selling animals to the public. It is administered by Pet Health Initiative, Inc. (PHI) and provides instruction on genetic screening as well as many other aspects of proper pet care. TEACH™-accredited sources screen animals for a variety of medical, behavioral and infectious diseases before they are sold. Project TEACH™ supports

29

the efforts of registries such as OFA, GDC and CERF and recommends that all animals sold be registered with the appropriate agencies. For more information on Project TEACH™, send a self-addressed stamped envelope to Pet Health Initiative, P.O. Box 12093, Scottsdale, AZ 85267-2093.

The Orthopedic Foundation for Animals (OFA) is a nonprofit organization established in 1966 to collect and disseminate information concerning orthopedic diseases of animals and to establish control programs to lower the incidence of orthopedic diseases in animals. A registry is maintained for both hip dysplasia and elbow dysplasia. The ultimate purpose of OFA certification is to provide information to dog owners to assist in the selection of good breeding animals. Therefore, attempts to get a dysplastic dog certified will only hurt the breed by perpetuation of the disease. For more information contact your veterinarian or the Orthopedic Foundation for Animals, 2300 Nifong Blvd., Columbia, MO 65201.

The Institute for Genetic Disease Control in Animals (GDC) is a nonprofit organization founded in 1990 and maintains an open registry for orthopedic problems but does not compete with OFA. In an open registry like GDC, owners, breeders, veterinarians, and scientists can trace the genetic history of any particular dog, once that dog and close relatives have been registered. At the present time, the GDC operates open registries for hip dysplasia, elbow dysplasia, and osteochondrosis. The GDC is currently developing guidelines for registries of: Legg-Calve-Perthes disease, craniomandibular osteopathy, and medial patellar luxation. For more information, contact the Institute for Genetic Disease Control in Animals, P.O. Box 222, Davis, CA 95617.

The Canine Eye Registration Foundation (CERF) is an international organization devoted to eliminating hereditary eye diseases from purebred dogs. This organization is similar to OFA that helps eliminate diseases like hip dysplasia. CERF is a nonprofit organization that screens and certifies purebreds as free of heritable eye diseases. Dogs are evaluated by veterinary eye specialists and findings are then submitted to CERF for documentation. The goal is to identify purebreds without heritable eye prob-

Rottweilers are very patient with the people they love and will do just about anything for family members. This is patience personified!

lems, so they can be used for breeding. Dogs being considered for breeding programs should be screened and certified by CERF on an annual basis, since not all problems are evident in puppies. For more information on CERF, write to CERF, SCC-A, Purdue University, West Lafayette, IN 47907.

FEEDING & NUTRITION

WHAT YOU MUST CONSIDER EVERY DAY TO FEED YOUR ROTTWEILER THROUGH HIS LIFETIME

Nutrition is one of the most important aspects of raising a healthy Rottweiler, and yet, it is often the source of much controversy between breeders, veterinarians, pet owners, and dog food manufacturers. However, most of these argu-ments have more to do with marketing than with science.

Facing page: Nutrition is very important, but Hanibal won't find it in a sand bucket. Owner, Barb McNinch.

Let's first take a look at dog foods and then determine the needs of our dog. This chapter will concentrate on feeding the pet Rottweiler rather than breeding or working Rottweilers.

COMMERCIAL DOG FOODS

Most dog foods are sold based on marketing (i.e., how to make a product appealing to owners while meeting the needs of dogs). Some foods are marketed on the basis of their protein content others based on a "special" ingredient and still others are sold because they don't contain certain ingredients (e.g., preservatives, soy). We want a dog food that specifically meets our dog's needs, is economical, and causes few if any problems. Most foods come in dry, semi-moist and canned forms. Some can now be purchased frozen. The "dry" foods are the most economical containing the least fat and the most preservatives. The canned foods are the most expensive (they're 75% water) usually containing the most fat and the least preservatives. Semi-moist foods are expensive, high in sugar content and I do not recommend them for any dogs.

When you're selecting a commercial diet, make sure the food has been assessed by feeding trials for a specific life stage, not just by nutrient analysis. This statement is usually located near the ingredient label. In the United States, these trials are performed in accordance with American Association of Feed Control Officials (AAFCO) and, in Canada, by the Canadian Veterinary Medical Association. This certification is important because it has been found that dog foods currently on the market that provide only a chemical analysis and calculated values, but no feeding trial, may not provide adequate nutrition. The feeding trials show that the diets meet minimal, not optimal, standards. However, they are the best tests we currently have.

PUPPY REQUIREMENTS

Soon after pups are born, and certainly within the first 24 hours, they should begin nursing from their mother. This provides them with colostrum, an antibody-rich milk that helps protect them from infection for their first few months of life. Pups should be allowed to nurse for at least six weeks before they are completely weaned from their mother. Supplemental feeding may be started by as early as three weeks of age.

By two months of age, pups should be fed puppy food. They are now in an important growth phase. Nutritional deficiencies and/or imbalances during this time of life are more devastating than at any other time. Also, this is not the time to overfeed pups or provide them with "performance" rations. Overfeeding Rottweilers can lead to serious skeletal defects such as osteochondrosis and hip dysplasia.

Pups should be fed "growth" diets until they are 12-18 months of age. Many Rottweilers do not mature until 18 months of age and so benefit from a longer period on these rations. Pups will initially need to be fed two to three meals daily until they are 12-18 months old, then once to twice daily (preferably twice) when they are converted to adult food. Proper growth diets should be selected based on acceptable feeding trials designed for growing pups. If you can't tell by reading the label, ask your veterinarian for feeding advice.

Remember that pups need "balance" in their diets and avoid the temptation to supplement with protein, vitamins, or

Making fresh, clean water available to your Rottweiler at all times is important to his health. Rottweilers can dehydrate very easily.

minerals. Calcium supplements have been implicated as a cause of bone and cartilage deformity, especially in large breed puppies. Puppy diets are already heavily fortified with calcium, and supplements tend to unbalance the mineral intake. There is more than adequate proof that these supplements are responsible for many bone deformities seen in these growing dogs.

ADULT DIETS

The goal of feeding adult dogs is one of "maintenance." They have already done all the grow-

Adult Rottweilers need a balanced diet and exercise to keep them in proper condition and at the correct weight.

ing they are going to do and are unlikely to have the digestive problems of elderly dogs. In general, dogs can do well on maintenance rations containing predominantly plant- or animal-based ingredients as long as that ration has been specifically formulated to meet maintenance level requirements. This contention should be supported by studies performed by the manufacturer in accordance with AAFCO (American Association of Feed Control Officials). In Canada, these products should be certified by the Canadian Veterinary Medical Association to meet maintenance requirements.

There's nothing wrong with feeding a cereal-based diet to dogs on maintenance rations, and they are the most economical. Soy is a common ingredient in cereal-based diets but may not be completely digested by all dogs, especially Rottweilers. This causes no medical problems, although Rottweilers may tend to be more flatulent on these diets. When comparing maintenance rations, it must be appreciated that these diets must meet the "minimal" requirements for confined dogs, not necessarily optimal levels. Most dogs will benefit when fed diets that contain easily-digested ingredients that provide nutrients at least slightly above minimum requirements. Typically, these foods will be intermediate in price between the most expensive super-premium diets and the cheapest generic diets. Select only those diets that have been substantiated by feeding trials to meet maintenance requirements, those that contain wholesome ingredients, and those recommended by your veterinarian. Don't select based on price alone, on company advertising, or on total protein content.

GERIATRIC DIETS

Rottweilers are considered elderly when they are about seven years of age, and there are certain changes that occur as dogs age that alter their nutritional requirements. As pets age, their metabolism slows and this must be accounted for. If maintenance rations are fed in the same amounts while metabolism is slowing, weight gain may result. Obesity is the last thing one wants to contend with in an elderly pet since it increases their risk of several other health-related problems. As pets age, most of their organs do not function as well as in youth. The digestive system, liver, pancreas, and gallbladder are not functioning at peak effect. The intestines have more difficulty extracting all the nutrients from the food consumed. A gradual decline in kidney function is considered a normal part of aging.

A responsible approach to geriatric nutrition is to realize that degenerative changes are a normal part of aging. Our goal is to minimize the potential damage done by taking this into account while the dog is still well. If we wait until an elderly dog is ill before we change the diet, we have a much harder job.

Elderly dogs need to be treated as individuals. While some benefit from the nutrition found in "senior" diets, others might do better on the highly-digestible puppy and super-premium diets. These latter diets provide an excellent blend of digestibility and amino acid content, but unfortunately, many are higher in salt and phosphorus than the older pet really needs.

Older dogs are also more prone to developing arthritis, and therefore, it is important not to overfeed them since obesity puts added stress on the joints. For animals with joint pain, supplementing the diet with fatty acid combinations containing cis-linoleic acid, gamma-linolenic acid and eicosapentaenoic acid can be quite beneficial.

MEDICAL CONDITIONS AND DIET

It is important to keep in mind that dietary choices can affect the development of orthopedic diseases such as hip dysplasia and osteochondrosis. When feeding a pup at risk, avoid high-calorie diets and try to feed several times a day rather than ad libitum. Sudden growth spurts are to be avoided because they result in joint instability. Recent research has also suggested that the electrolyte balance of the diet may also play a role in the development of hip dysplasia. Rations that had more balance between the positively and negatively charged elements in the diet (e.g., sodium, potassium, chloride) were less likely to promote hip dysplasia in susceptible dogs. Also avoid supplements of calcium, phosphorus and vitamin D as they can interfere with normal bone and cartilage development. The fact is that calcium levels in the body are carefully regulated by hormones (such as calcitonin and parathormone) as well as vitamin D. Supplementation disturbs this normal regulation and can cause many problems. It has also been shown that calcium supplementation can interfere with the proper absorption of zinc from the intestines. If you really feel the need to supplement your dog, select products such as eicosapentaenoic/gamma-linolenic fatty acid combinations or small amounts of vitamin C.

Diet can't prevent bloat (gastric dilatation/volvulus) but changing feeding habits can make a difference. Initially, the bloat occurs when the stomach becomes distended with swallowed air. This air is swallowed as a consequence of gulping food or water, stress and exercising too close to mealtime. This is where we can make a difference. Divide meals and feed them three times daily rather than all at once. Soak dry dog food in water before feeding to decrease the tendency to gulp the food. If you want to feed dry food only, add some large clean chew toys to the feed bowl so that the dog has to "pick" to get at the food and can't gulp it. Putting the food bowl on a stepstool, so the dog doesn't have to stretch to get the food, may also be helpful. Finally, don't allow any exercise for at least one hour before and after feeding.

Fat supplements are probably the most common supplements purchased from pet supply stores. They frequently promise to add luster, gloss, and sheen to the coat and consequently make dogs look healthy. The only fatty acid that is essential for this purpose is cis-linoleic acid, which is found in flaxseed oil, sunflower seed oil, and safflower oil. Corn oil is a suitable but less effective alternative. Most of the other oils found in retail supplements are high in saturated and monounsaturated fats and are not beneficial for shiny fur or healthy skin. For dogs with allergies, arthritis, high blood pressure (hypertension), high cholesterol, and some heart ailments, other fatty acids may be prescribed by a veterinarian. The important ingredients in these products are gamma-linolenic acid (GLA), eicosapentaenoic acid (EPA), and docosahexaenoic acid (DHA). These products have gentle and natural anti-inflammatory properties, but don't be fooled by imitations. Most retail fatty acid supplements do not contain these functional forms of the essential fatty acids—look for gamma-linolenic acid, eicosapentaenoic acid, and docosahexaenoic acid on the label.

Supplementing normal feeding can be dangerous to your dog's health. Avoid calcium, phosphorus and vitamin D — but a little vitamin C doesn't hurt. Breeder, Dr. Margaret Zazzaro.

HEALTH

**PREVENTIVE MEDICINE AND HEALTH
CARE FOR YOUR ROTTWEILER**

Keeping your Rottweiler healthy requires preventive health care. This is not only the most effective but the least expensive way to battle illness. Good preventive care starts even before puppies are born.  The dam should be well cared for, vacci-nated, and free of infections and para-sites. Hopefully, both parents were screened for impor-

Facing page: Noblehaus Quelle Image, CGC and progeny Zobel Bone in the USA V. Noblehaus CD, CGC, TDI, owned by Randy and Trish Helsdon, are prime examples of good health.

tant genetic diseases, registered with the appropriate agencies (e.g., OFA, GDC, CERF), showed no evidence of medical or behavioral problems and were found to be good candidates for breeding. This gives the pup a good start in life. If all has been planned well, the dam will pass on resistance to disease to her pups that will last for the first few months of life. However, the

At six to eight weeks of age your Rottweiler puppy should be checked out by a veterinarian for everything from wandering knee caps to heart murmurs.

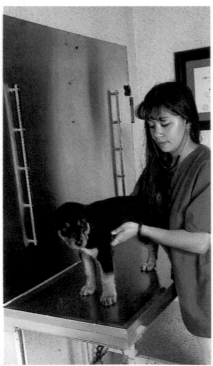

dam can also pass on parasites, infections, genetic diseases and more.

TWO TO THREE WEEKS OF AGE

By two to three weeks of life, it is usually necessary to start pups on a regimen to control worms. Although dogs benefit from this parasite control, the primary reason for doing this is human health. After whelping, the dam often sheds large numbers of worms even if she tested negative previously. This is because many worms lay dormant in tissues, and the stress of delivery causes parasite release into the environment. Assume that all puppies potentially have worms because studies have shown that 75% do. Thus, we institute worm control early to protect the people in the house from worms more than the pups themselves. The deworming is repeated every two to three weeks until your veterinarian feels the condition is under control. Nursing bitches should be treated at the same time because they often shed worms during this time. Only use products recommended by your veterinarian. Over-the-counter parasiticides have been responsible for deaths in pups.

SIX TO TWENTY WEEKS OF AGE

Most puppies are weaned from their mother at six to eight weeks of age. Weaning shouldn't be done too early so that pups have the opportunity to socialize with their littermates and dam. This is important for them to be able to respond to other dogs later in life. There is no reason to rush the weaning process unless the dam can't produce enough milk to feed the pups.

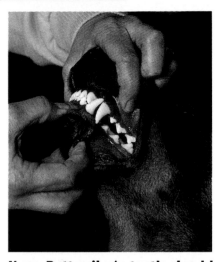

Your Rottweiler's teeth should be checked regularly by your veterinarian. Follow his instructions for home dental care and always provide your Rottweiler with a properly sized Nylabone®.

Pups are usually first examined by their veterinarian at six to eight weeks of age, which is when most vaccination schedules commence. If pups are exposed to many other dogs at this young age, veterinarians often opt for vaccinating with inactivated parvovirus at six weeks of age. When exposure isn't a factor, most veterinarians would rather wait to see the pup at eight weeks of age. At this point, they can also do a preliminary dental evaluation to see that all the puppy teeth are coming in correctly, check to see that the testicles are properly descending in males, and that there are no health reasons to prohibit vaccination at this time. Heart murmurs, wandering knee-caps (luxating patellae), juvenile cataracts, persistent pupillary membranes (a congenital eye disease), and hernias are usually evident by this time.

Your veterinarian may also be able to perform temperament testing on the pup by eight weeks of age, or recommend someone to do it for you. Although temperament testing is not completely accurate, it can often predict which pups are most anxious and fearful. Some form of temperament evaluation is important because behavioral problems account for more animals being euthanized (killed) each year than all medical conditions combined.

43

Recently, some veterinary hospitals have been recommending neutering pups as early as six to eight weeks of age. A study done at the University of Florida College of Veterinary Medicine over a span of more than four years concluded there was no increase in complications when animals were neutered at less than six months of age. The evaluators also concluded that the surgery appeared to be less stressful when done in young pups.

Most vaccination schedules consist of injections being given at 6-8, 10-12, and 14-16 weeks of age. Ideally, vaccines should not be given closer than two weeks apart, and three to four weeks seems to be optimal. Each vaccine usually consists of several different viruses (e.g., parvovirus, distemper, parainfluenza, hepatitis) combined into one injection. Coronavirus can be given as a separate vaccination according to this same schedule if pups are at risk. Some veterinarians and breeders advise another parvovirus booster at 18-20 weeks of age. A booster is given for all vaccines at one year of age and annually thereafter. For animals at increased risk of exposure, parvovirus vaccination may be given as often as four times a year. A new vaccine for canine cough (tracheobronchitis) is squirted into the nostrils. It can be given as early as six weeks of age if pups are at risk. Leptospirosis vaccination is given in some geographic areas and likely offers protection for six to eight months. The initial series consists of three to four injections spaced two to three weeks apart, starting as early as ten weeks of age. Rabies vaccine is given as a separate injection at three months of age, then repeated when the pup is one year old, then every one to three years depending on local risk and government regulation.

Some dogs have difficulty mounting a complete and protective response to vaccinations, especially Rottweilers. In these cases, we typically recommend running a test to measure antibody titer (level) for parvovirus at 16 weeks of age and annually thereafter. This helps ensure that the vaccinations that are given will, in fact, be protective.

A high-titer parvovirus vaccine, recently introduced in North America, is recommended for pups 6 to 18 weeks of age and does not interfere with the dam's protection. Nonetheless, certain lines of Rottweilers and Dobermans have proven low or poor responders and may still be unable to mount a protective response.

Between eight and fourteen weeks of age, use every opportunity to expose the pup to as many people and situations as possible. This is part of the critical socialization period that will determine how good a pet your dog will become. This is not the time to abandon a puppy for eight hours while you go to work. This is also not the time to punish your dog in any way, shape or form.

This is the time to introduce your dog to neighborhood cats, birds and other creatures. Hold off on exposure to other dogs until after the second vaccination in the series. You don't want your new friend to pick up contagious diseases from dogs it meets in its travels before it has adequate protection. By 12 weeks of age, your pup should be ready for social outings with other dogs. Do it! It's a great way for your dog to feel comfortable around members of its own species. Walk the streets and introduce your pup to everybody you meet. Your goal should be to introduce your dog to every type of person or situation it is likely to encounter in its life. Take it in cars, elevators, buses, subways, to parade grounds and beaches; you want it to habituate to all environments. Expose your pup to kids, teenagers, old people, people in wheelchairs, people on bicycles, people in uniforms. The more varied the

Once-a-month oral medications help prevent heartworm as well as many of the common intestinal parasites, such as hookworms, roundworms, and whipworms.

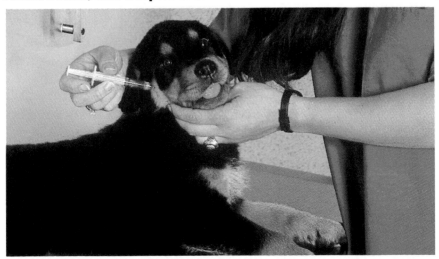

exposure, the better the socialization.

Proper identification of your pet is also important since it minimizes the risk of theft and increases the chances that your pet will be returned to you if it is lost. There are several different options. Microchip implantation is a relatively painless procedure involving the subcutaneous injection of an implant the size of a grain of rice. This implant does not act as a beacon if your pet is missing. However, if your pet turns up at a veterinary clinic or shelter and is checked with a scanner, the chip provides information about you that can be used to quickly reunite you with your pet. This method of identification is reasonably priced, permanent in nature, and performed at most veterinary clinics. Another option is tattooing, which can be done on the inner ear or on the skin of the abdomen. Most purebreds are given a number by the associated registry (e.g., American Kennel Club, The Kennel Club, United Kennel Club, Canadian Kennel Club, etc.) that is used for identification. Alternatively, permanent numbers such as social security numbers (telephone numbers and addresses may change during the life of your pet) can be used in the tattooing

process. There are several different tattoo registries maintaining lists of dogs, their tattoo codes and their owners. Finally, identifying collars and tags provide quick information but can be separated from your pet if it is lost or stolen. They work best when combined with a permanent identification system such as microchip implantation or tattooing.

FOUR TO TWELVE MONTHS OF AGE

At 16 weeks of age, when your pup gets the last in its series of regular induction vaccinations, ask your veterinarian about evaluating the pup for hip dysplasia with the PennHip™ technique. This helps predict the risk of developing hip dysplasia as well as degenerative joint disease. Since anesthesia is typically required for the procedure, many veterinarians like to do the evaluation at the same time as neutering. This is also a great time to run the parvovirus antibody titer to determine how well your dog has responded to the vaccination series.

As a general rule, neuter your animal at about six months of age unless you fully intend to breed it. As we know, neutering can be safely done at eight weeks of age but this is still not a com-

After neutering, your Rottweiler is bound to be bedridden for a couple of days. Six months old is the ideal age to have this procedure done.

mon practice. Neutering not only stops the possibility of pregnancy and undesirable behaviors but can prevent several health problems as well. It is a well-established fact that female pups spayed before their first heat have a dramatically reduced incidence of mammary (breast) cancer. Likewise, neutered males significantly decrease their incidence of prostate disorders.

When your pet is six months of age, your veterinarian will want to take a blood sample to perform a heartworm test. If the test is negative and shows no evidence of heartworm infection, the pup will go on heartworm prevention therapy. Some veterinarians are even recommending preventive therapy in younger pups. This might be a once-a-day regimen, but newer therapies can be given on a once-a-month basis. As a bonus, most of these heartworm preventatives also help prevent internal parasites.

Another part of the six month visit should be a thorough dental evaluation to make sure all the permanent teeth have correctly erupted. If they haven't, this will be the time to correct the problem. Correction should only be performed to make the animal more comfortable and promote normal chewing. The procedures should never be used to cosmetically improve the appearance of a dog used for show purposes or breeding.

After the dental evaluation, you should start implementing home dental care. In most cases, this will consist of brushing the teeth one or more times each week and perhaps using dental rinses. It is a sad fact that 85% of dogs over four years of age have periodontal disease and "doggy breath." In fact, it is so common that most people think it is "normal." Well, it is normal—as normal as bad breath would be in people if they never brushed their teeth. Brush your dog's teeth regularly with a special tooth brush and toothpaste and you can greatly reduce the incidence of tartar buildup, bad breath and gum disease. Provide the Puppy Bone™ from Nylabone® and a Gumabone® to puppies as early as eight to ten weeks. Nylabones® not only help in the proper development of the puppy's jaw and the emergence of adult teeth but help to keep the teeth clean...and the breath fresh. Better preventive care means that dogs live a long time and they'll enjoy their sunset years more if they still have their teeth. Ask your veterinarian for details on home dental care.

THE FIRST SEVEN YEARS

At one year of age, your dog should be re-examined and have boosters for all vaccines. Your veterinarian will also

Yuck! Doggy breath! Be sure to keep your Rottweiler's teeth clean to prevent disease and bad breath.

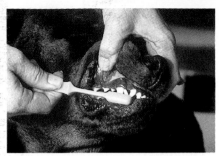

One good way to keep your Rottweiler's teeth clean is weekly brushing with special tartar-reducing toothpaste made especially for dogs.

graphs (x-rays) of the hips and elbows to look for evidence of dysplastic changes. Remind your veterinarian to also take radiographs of the tarsocrural joint since this form of osteochondrosis is most commonly seen in the Rottweiler. Genetic Disease Control (GDC) will certify hips and elbows at 12 months of age; Orthopedic Foundation for Animals (OFA) won't issue certification until 24 months of age.

want to do a very thorough physical examination to look for early evidence of problems. This might include taking radio-

At any age, your Rottweiler is prone to heat exhaustion and sunstroke — take the proper precautions and dress appropriately.

Nylafloss® is a durable nylon tug toy that flosses his teeth while he plays with it. Never buy cotton tug toys, as cotton is organic and rots.

At 12 months of age, it's also a great time to have some blood samples analyzed to provide background information. Although few Rottweilers experience clinical hypothyroidism at this young age, the process may be starting. Therefore, it is a good idea to have baseline levels of thyroid hormones (free and total), TSH, blood cell counts, organ chemistries, parvovirus antibody titers and cholesterol levels. This can serve as a valuable comparison to samples collected in the future.

Each year, preferably around the time of your pet's birthday, it's time for another veterinary visit. This visit is a wonderful opportunity for a thorough clinical examination rather than just "shots." Since 85% of dogs have periodontal disease by four years of age, veterinary intervention

Rottweilers are prone to a few eye diseases and should be inspected by a veterinarian at least once a year. Regularly check for signs of persistent cloudiness or opacity on the lens.

does not seem to be as widespread as it should be. The examination should include visually inspecting the ears, eyes (a great time to start scrutinizing for progressive retinal atrophy, cataracts, etc.), mouth (don't wait for gum disease), and groin; listening (auscultation) to the lungs and heart; feeling (palpating) the lymph nodes and abdomen and answering all of

your questions about optimal health care. In addition, booster vaccinations are given during these times, feces are checked for parasites, urine is analyzed, and blood samples may be collected for analysis. One of the tests run on the blood sample is for heartworm antigen. In areas of the country where heartworm is only present in the spring, summer and fall (it's spread by mosquitoes), blood samples are collected and evaluated about a month prior to the mosquito season. Other routine blood tests are for blood cells (hematology), organ chemistries, thyroid levels and electrolytes.

By two years of age, most veterinarians prefer to begin preventive dental cleanings often referred to as "prophies." Anesthesia is required and the veterinarian or veterinary dentist will use an ultrasonic scaler to remove plaque and tartar from above and below the gum line as well as polish the teeth so that plaque has a harder time sticking to them. Radiographs (x-rays) and fluoride treatments are other options. It is now known that it is plaque, not tartar, that initiates inflammation in the gums. Since scaling and root planing remove more tartar than plaque, veterinary dentists have begun using a new technique called PerioBUD (periodontal bactericidal ultrasonic debridement). The ultrasonic treatment is quicker, disrupts more bacteria and is less irritating to the gums. With tooth polishing to finish up the procedure, gum healing is better and owners can start home care sooner. Each dog has its own dental needs that must be addressed, but most veterinary dentists recommend prophies annually. Be sure too that your Rottweiler always has a Nylabone® available to do his part in keeping his teeth clean.

SENIOR ROTTWEILERS

Rottweilers are considered seniors when they reach about seven years of age. Veterinarians still usually only need to examine them once a year, but it is now important to start screening for geriatric problems. Accordingly, blood profiles, urinalysis, chest radiographs (x-rays) and electrocardiograms (EKG) are recommended on an annual basis. When problems are caught early, they are much more likely to be successfully managed. This is as true in canine medicine as it is in human medicine.

During yearly check ups, the veterinarian will check the ears of your Rottweiler for parasites such as mites, which can cause mange.

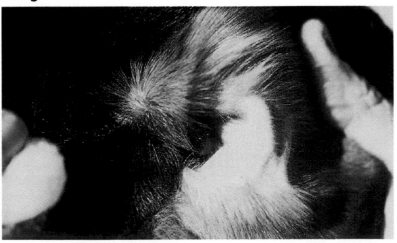

MEDICAL
PROBLEMS

**RECOGNIZED GENETIC CONDITIONS
SPECIFICALLY RELATED TO THE ROTTWEILER**

M any conditions appear to be especially prominent in Rottweilers. Sometimes it is possible to identify the genetic basis of a problem, but in many cases, we must be satisfied with merely identifying the breeds that are at risk and how the conditions can be identified, treated and pre-

Facing page: Your Rottweiler depends on you to know what's best for him. This vibrant champion is owned by Suzanne E. Burris.

vented. Following are some conditions that have been recognized as being common in the Rottweiler, but this listing is certainly not complete. Also, many genetic conditions may be common in certain breed lines, not in the breed in general.

AORTIC STENOSIS

Aortic stenosis is a congenital heart defect in which fibrous tissue impedes the flow of blood out of the heart. One of the breeds in which it is most commonly reported is the Rottweiler. Genetic studies have demonstrated that at least two genes are involved, one of which is autosomal dominant (only requires one parent to be the carrier). Some affected pups may seem fairly normal, while others show all the classic symptoms of heart failure. A family history is usually evident. Veterinarians may suspect the diagnosis based on hearing the classic heart murmur, but the diagnosis can be confirmed by ultrasound examination of the heart (echocardiography) and usually by radiography (x-rays) as well. There is no standard approach to treatment. Mildly affected animals usually require no treatment at all. Others may benefit from the use of beta-blockers to help control the symptoms (but not cure

the problem). More severely affected pups require heart surgery prior to six months of age, before permanent changes in the heart are evident. Affected animals, their siblings and parents should not be used in any breeding programs.

CRUCIATE LIGAMENT RUPTURE

The cruciate ligaments crisscross within the knee joint and serve an anchoring function. Rupture of the anterior cruciate ligament is very common in dogs and is one of the most common causes of hind-leg lameness in the young adult Rottweiler (two to six years of age). The lameness that results from cruciate ligament rupture is not always painful. Affected dogs may carry the leg for a while, but eventually start putting more weight on the leg. Unfortunately, although they may start using the leg, more damage is likely to occur in the knee as the body attempts to stabilize the joint. The condition can be diagnosed by manipulation of the knee with the animal anesthetized or it can be diagnosed and treated during arthroscopic surgery. Removing fluid from the joint for analysis (arthrocentesis) may also confirm the presence of a degenerative joint disorder. The standard treatment for rupture of the anterior cruciate ligament is surgery. In one study, 50% of Rottweilers with cranial cruciate rupture had involvement in both knees. Most veterinarians recommend bandage or cast support for two to six weeks after surgery to help support the joint while it heals. When the bandage or cast is finally removed, limited activity (e.g., leash walking) and physical therapy (e.g., swimming) are encouraged.

This tailed wonder is SP Razzmatazz Bulldozer owned by Marc Elmlund of Sweden. Tail docking is fast becoming unpopular on the whole Continent.

DEGENERATIVE MYELOPATHY

Degenerative myelopathy is a collection of slowly progressive degenerative disorders of the spinal cord. They are relatively rare, but the Rottweiler has the misfortune of being prone to two different varieties of the condition. In fact, they are both named for the breed because they have been reported in no other breeds.

Leukoencephalomyelopathy of Rottweilers is a demyelinating spinal cord and brain disease that usually first manifests itself in Rottweilers that are 1 to 3 years of age. The condition is slowly progressive over a period of months or years, and eventually, affected individuals develop spastic leg lameness.

Neuroaxonal dystrophy of Rottweilers is an autosomal recessive hereditary disorder in which "spheroids" appear throughout the brain and spinal cord. The end result is an awkward gait in all four limbs and a progressive head tremor.

Neither condition is curable, although some animals do respond to appropriate supportive care. Obviously these animals should not be used for breeding and neither should their siblings or parents.

ELBOW DYSPLASIA

Elbow dysplasia doesn't refer to just one disease, but rather an entire complex of disorders that affect the elbow joint. Several different processes might be involved, including ununited anconeal process, fragmented medial coronoid process, osteochondritis of the medial humeral condyle, or incomplete ossification of the humeral condyle. Elbow dysplasia and osteochondrosis are disorders of young dogs, with problems usually starting between four and seven months of age. The usual manifestation is a sudden onset of lameness. In time, the continued inflammation results in arthritis in those affected joints. Statistics compiled by the Or-

Rottweilers are fast-growing, large dogs. A diet high in calories, calcium and protein may contribute to the development of diseases linked with elbow dysplasia in the Rottweiler.

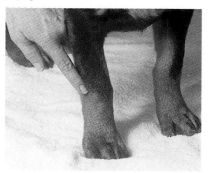

thopedic Foundation for Animals found that 47.9% of male Rottweilers and 38.1% of female Rottweilers assessed up until December 31, 1994 have evidence of elbow dysplasia on radiographs (x-rays). Continued registration is critical to allow lowering the extremely high incidence of this disorder in Rottweilers.

Radiographs (x-rays) are taken of the elbow joints and submitted to a registry for evaluation. The Orthopedic Foundation for Animals (OFA) will assign a breed registry number to those animals with normal elbows that are over 24 months of age. Abnormal elbows are reported as Grade I to III, where Grade III elbows have well-developed degenerative joint disease (arthritis). Normal elbows on individuals 24 months or older are assigned a breed registry number and are periodically reported to parent breed clubs. Genetic Disease Control for Animals (GDC) maintains an open registry for elbow dysplasia and assigns a registry number to those individuals with normal elbows at 12 months of age or older. Only animals with "normal" elbows should be used for breeding.

There is strong evidence to support the contention that OCD

of the elbow is an inherited disease, likely controlled by many genes. A hereditary basis for the disease has been definitively proven in the Rottweiler. Preliminary research (in Labrador Retrievers) also suggests that the different forms of elbow dysplasia are inherited independently. Therefore, breeding stock should be selected from those animals without a history of osteochondrosis, preferably for several generations. Unaffected dogs producing offspring with OCD, FCP, or both should not be bred again and unaffected first-degree relatives (e.g., siblings) should not be used for breeding either.

The most likely associations made to date suggest that, other than genetics, feeding diets high in calories, calcium and protein promote the development of osteochondrosis in susceptible dogs. Also, animals that are allowed to exercise in an unregulated fashion are at increased risk, since they are more likely to sustain cartilage injuries.

The management of dogs with OCD is a matter of much debate and controversy. Some recommend surgery to remove the damaged cartilage before permanent damage is done. Others recommend conservative therapy of rest and pain-killers. The most common drugs used are aspirin and polysulfated glycosaminoglycans. Most veterinarians agree that the use of cortisone-like compounds (corticosteroids) creates more problems than it treats in this condition. What seems clear, is that some dogs will respond to conservative therapies, while others need surgery. Surgery is often helpful if performed before there is significant joint damage.

GASTRIC DILATATION/ VOLVULUS

Gastric dilatation (bloat) occurs when the stomach becomes distended with air. The air gets swallowed into the stomach when susceptible dogs exercise, gulp their food/water or are stressed. Although bloat can occur at any age, it becomes more common as susceptible dogs get older. Purebreds are three times more likely to suffer from bloat than mutts. Although Rottweilers are susceptible to the condition and frequently appear in lists of "breeds most prone to bloat," recent large surveys have found that Rottweilers are not as prone as other deep-chested breeds such as Great Danes, Weimaraners, Saint Bernards, Gordon Setters, Irish Setters, Boxers and Standard Poodles.

Bloat on its own is uncomfortable, but it is the possible consequences that make it life-threatening. As the stomach fills with air like a balloon, it can twist on itself and impede the flow of food within the stomach as well as the blood supply to the stomach and other digestive organs. This twisting (volvulus or torsion) not only makes the bloat worse, but also results in toxins being released into the bloodstream and death of blood-deprived tissues. These events, if allowed to progress, will usually result in death in four to six hours. Approximately one-third of dogs with bloat and volvulus will die, even under appropriate hospital care.

Affected dogs will be uncomfortable, restless, depressed and have an extended abdomen. They need veterinary attention immediately or they will suffer from shock and die! There are a variety of surgical procedures to correct the abnormal positioning of the stomach and organs. Intensive medical therapy is also necessary to treat for shock, acidosis and the effects of toxins.

Bloat can't be completely prevented, but there are some easy things to do to greatly reduce risk. Don't leave food down for dogs to eat as they wish. Divide the day's meals into three portions and feed morning, after-

noon and evening. Try not to let your dog gulp its food; if necessary, add some chew toys to the bowl so he has to work around them to get the food. Add water to dry food before feeding. Have fresh, clean water available all day but not at mealtime. Do not allow exercise for one hour before and after meals. Following this feeding advice may actually save your dog's life. In addition, there has been no studies that support the contention that soy in the diet increases the risk of bloat. Soy is relatively poorly digested and can lead to flatulence, but the gas accumulation in bloat comes from swallowed air, not gas produced in the intestines.

HIP DYSPLASIA

Hip dysplasia is a genetically transmitted developmental problem of the hip joint that is common in many breeds. Dogs may be born with a "susceptibility" or "tendency" to develop hip dysplasia, but it is not a foregone conclusion that all susceptible dogs will eventually develop hip dysplasia. All dysplastic dogs are born with normal hips and the dysplastic changes begin within the first 24 months of life, although they are usually evident long before then.

It is now known that there are

several factors that help determine whether a susceptible dog will ever develop hip dysplasia. These include body size, conformation, growth patterns, caloric load and electrolyte balance in the dog food.

Rottweilers are often cited as being prone to hip dysplasia. Based on research tabulated up to January, 1995, the Orthopedic Foundation for Animals concluded that 22% of the radiographs submitted from Rottweilers had evidence of hip dysplasia. This reflects a decrease in the breed incidence of 20-30% since the 1970s. This is great news, but Rottweiler breeders are still a long way from ridding their lines of dysplastic dogs.

When purchasing a Rottweiler pup, it is best to ensure that the parents were both registered with normal hips through one of the international registries, such as the Orthopedic Foundation for Animals or Genetic Disease Control. Pups over 16 weeks of age can be tested by veterinarians trained in the PennHip™ procedure, which is a way of predicting risk of developing hip dysplasia and arthritis. In time, it should be possible to virtually eradicate hip dysplasia from the breed.

If you start with a pup with less risk of hip dysplasia, you

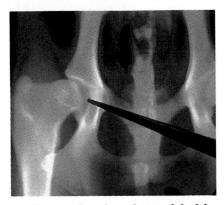

Radiograph of a dog with hip dysplasia. Note the flattened femoral head at the marker. Courtesy of Toronto Academy of Veterinary Medicine, Toronto, Canada.

can further reduce your risk by controlling its environment. Select a food with a moderate amount of protein and avoid the super high premium and high-calorie diets. Also, feed your pup several times a day for defined periods (e.g., 15 minutes) rather than leaving the food down all day. Avoid all nutritional supplements, especially those that include calcium, phosphorus and/or vitamin D. Use controlled exercise for your pup rather than letting him run loose. Unrestricted exercise in the pup can stress the joints, which are still developing.

If you have a dog with hip dysplasia, all is not lost. There is much variability in the clinical presentation. Some dogs with severe dysplasia experience little pain, while others that have minor changes may be extremely sore. The main problem is that dysplastic hips promote degenerative joint disease (osteoarthritis or osteoarthrosis) which can eventually incapacitate the joint. Aspirin and other anti-inflammatory agents are suitable in the early stages; surgery is needed when animals are in great pain, when drug therapy doesn't work adequately, or when movement is severely compromised.

HYPOTHYROIDISM

Hypothyroidism is the most commonly diagnosed endocrine (hormonal) problem in the Rottweiler. The disease itself refers to an insufficient amount of thyroid hormones being produced. Although there are several different potential causes, lymphocytic thyroiditis is by far the most common. Iodine deficiency and goiter are extremely rare. In lymphocytic thyroiditis, the body produces antibodies that target aspects of thyroid tissue; the process usually starts between one and three years of age in affected animals but doesn't become clinically evident until later in life.

There is a great deal of misinformation about hypothyroidism. Owners often expect their dog to be obese and otherwise don't suspect the condition. The fact is that hypothyroidism is quite variable in its manifestations, and obesity is only seen in a small percentage of cases. In most cases, affected animals appear fine until they use up most of their remaining thyroid hormone reserves. The most common manifestations then are lack of energy and recurrent infections. Hair loss is seen in about one-third of cases.

You might suspect that hypothyroidism would be easy to diagnose but it is trickier than you think. Since there is a large reserve of thyroid hormones in the body, a test measuring only total blood levels of the hormones (T-4 and T-3) is not a very sensitive indicator of the condition. Thyroid stimulation tests are the best way to measure the functional reserve. Measuring "free" and "total" levels of the hormones and endogenous TSH (thyroid-stimulating hormone) are other approaches. Also, since we know that most cases are due to antibodies produced in the body, screening for these autoantibodies can help identify animals at risk of developing hypothyroidism.

Because this breed is so prone

to developing hypothyroidism, periodic "screening" for the disorder is warranted in many cases. Although none of the screening tests is perfect, a basic panel evaluating total T-4, free T-4, TSH and cholesterol levels is a good start. Ideally, this would first be performed at one year of age and annually thereafter. This "screening" is practical because none of these tests is very expensive.

Fortunately, although there may be some problems in diagnosing hypothyroidism, treatment is straightforward and relatively inexpensive. Supplementing the affected animal twice daily with thyroid hormones effectively treats the condition. In many breeds, supplementation with thyroid hormones is commonly done to help confirm the diagnosis. Animals with hypothyroidism should not be used in a breeding program, and those with circulating autoantibodies but no actual hypothyroid disease should also not be used for breeding.

OSTEOCHONDROSIS

Osteochondrosis is a degenerative condition of cartilage, seen in young dogs, in which the cartilage cells fail to develop properly into mature bone. This results in localized areas of thickened cartilage that are very prone to injury since they are not well attached to the underlying bone. Therefore, although the condition is called osteochondrosis, which means a degenerative condition of bone and cartilage, this is essentially a disorder affecting cartilage, not bone.

In time, when osteochondrosis causes flaps of cartilage to be exposed in the joint, inflammation results. At this time, it is referred to as osteochondritis dissecans (OCD), describing the inflammatory component and the fact that cartilage has become "dissected" and exposed.

The factors that cause osteochondrosis are many but trauma, poor nutrition, and hereditary abnormalities have all been explored. The most likely associations made to date suggest that feeding diets high in calories, calcium and protein promote the development of osteochondrosis in susceptible dogs. Also, animals that are allowed to exercise in an unregulated fashion are at increased risk, since they are more likely to sustain cartilage injuries.

Osteochondrosis is a disorder of young Rottweilers, with problems usually starting between four and seven months of age. In the early stages of osteochon–

drosis, there are usually no clinical signs (symptoms). Only when a cleft forms in the cartilage and inflammation ensues is the condition clinically evident. The usual manifestation is a sudden onset of lameness. In time, the continued inflammation results in arthritis in those affected joints.

OCD of the head of the humerus (shoulder) is probably the most common manifestation of this condition in dogs. Most cases are seen in pups less than seven months of age, but one-third of cases are not detected until a year of age. The classic picture is one of lameness, and usually only one leg is involved initially. Both front legs eventually become involved in about 50% of cases. In time, if the problem is not addressed, the joint eventually becomes incapacitated with arthritis.

Osteochondrosis of the elbow is divided into ununited anconeal process, fragmented coronoid process and OCD of the medial humeral condyle. This triad of disorders is usually referred to by breeders collectively as elbow dysplasia and is covered here as a separate topic.

Osteochondrosis of the hind legs is much less common than the disease of the front legs. Some cases heal spontaneously, which may explain in part why it is more rarely reported. This condition (OCD of the hock or stifle) is most commonly seen the Rottweiler and so it is of some significance to us.

The diagnosis of OCD is often strongly suspected when a young dog of a breed at risk suddenly becomes painfully lame. Careful manipulation by a veterinarian can usually pinpoint the site of the problem. Radiographic

Letting your Rottweiler run around unrestricted increases his chance of developing elbow dysplasia because he is more likely to damage cartilage.

studies (x-rays) of the joints are very useful for establishing a diagnosis. If finances allow, it is worthwhile to take radiographs of both limbs for comparison purposes. Radiographs should also be taken of other joints on the same limb (e.g., elbow, shoulder, stifle) to evaluate for other potential sites of involvement. Radiographs are also necessary to diagnose OCD of the hind legs. Flap lesions of the hock (tarsocrural) joint are most common in the Rottweiler, but difficult to visualize in this breed because other anatomic structures are usually in the way. OCD flaps in this joint often contain bone, in contrast to OCD flaps in other joints which usually contain cartilage. If facilities allow, arthroscopic surgery can be used to diagnose and treat OCD of the hind legs.

The management of dogs with OCD is a matter of much debate and controversy. Some recommend surgery before permanent damage is done. Others recommend conservative therapy of rest and pain-killers. Each side has proponents. What seems clear, is that some dogs will respond to conservative therapies, while others need surgery. Polysulfated glycosaminoglycan (PSGSG) is a natural product with claims of protecting and repairing cartilage. It is being used experimentally in dogs and is not yet licensed for use in this species. Usually it is given as an intramuscular injection every four days for six doses, and then every four to six weeks as needed.

PRIMARY CILIARY DYSKINESIA

Primary ciliary dyskinesia, also known as immotile cilia syndrome and Kartagener's syndrome, refers to a condition in which the hair-like cilia in the respiratory passages cannot perform their needed defense mechanisms. The result is chronic respiratory infections. Since the tail of sperm are modified cilia, the condition can result in infertility as well. Primary ciliary dyskinesia is believed to be inherited in people as an autosomal recessive trait, but the genetics have not been confirmed in the dog.

The most common clinical manifestation of ciliary dyskinesia is recurring chronic respiratory infection. Therefore, affected dogs often cough, may develop a runny nose, have poor exercise tolerance, and sometimes fever. The result is often bronchitis and pneumonia. The tails (flagellae) of sperm are modified cilia so it is not surprising that many dogs with primary ciliary dyskinesia are infertile.

Approximately half of affected dogs have internal organs that are transposed to the wrong side of the body. Some affected individuals also have hearing loss, middle ear infections, and dysfunction of some of their white blood cells (neutrophils) needed to fight off infection.

The best way to confirm a diagnosis of primary ciliary dyskinesia is with special biopsies submitted for electron microscope evaluation or mucociliary clearance with a radiation counter. Both are involved procedures. In most cases, the diagnosis is suspected when a young animal gets recurrent respiratory infections that respond to antibiotics, but recur soon after the drug is discontinued. With mature intact males, sperm can be evaluated for defective sperm motility. This is not an absolute test because some dogs may have normal-appearing sperm yet still have the condition. In about 50% of cases, chest radiographs will reveal the heart on the right side of the chest.

There is no cure for primary ciliary dyskinesia. Symptomatic therapy includes periodic antibiotics based on culture results. Cough suppressants should not be used since they further impede normal defense mechanisms. If the infections can be maintained under reasonable control, affected dogs stand a chance of living a relatively normal existence. Affected dogs, their littermates and their parents should not be used in breeding programs.

PROGRESSIVE RETINAL ATROPHY (PRA)

Progressive retinal atrophy (PRA) refers to several inherited disorders affecting the retina that result in blindness. PRA is thought to be inherited with each breed demonstrating a specific age of onset and pattern of inheritance. These specifics have not yet been conclusively documented for the Rottweiler.

All of the conditions described as progressive retinal atrophy have one thing in common. There is progressive atrophy or degeneration of the retinal tissue. Visual impairment occurs slowly but progressively. Therefore, animals often adapt to their reduced vision until it is compromised to near blindness. Because of this, owners may not notice any visual impairment until the condition has progressed significantly.

Progressive retinal atrophy encompasses both degenerative and dysplastic varieties. This dis-

Rottweilers diagnosed with progressive retinal atrophy will eventually go blind because there is no cure for the disease. Retinal dysplasia is the variety that is most often seen in the Rottweiler.

tinction may seem confusing to owners, but it is important to remember that there are many distinctly different disorders that can result in PRA. Retinal dysplasia refers to malformation in the retinal tissue during fetal development, which is the variety seen most often in the Rottweiler.

The diagnosis of PRA can be made in two ways: direct visualization of the retina and electroretinography (ERG). When the ophthalmologist views the retina with an indirect ophthalmoscope, they can frequently see changes in the pattern of retinal blood vessels and the optic nerve which allow a diagnosis. The other highly sensitive test, usually available only from specialists is electroretinography. This instrument measures

electrical patterns in the retina and is sensitive enough to detect even the early onset of disease.

Unfortunately, there is no treatment available for progressive retinal atrophy and affected dogs will eventually go blind. Fortunately, PRA is not a painful condition, and dogs do have other keen senses upon which they can depend. Prevention is possible since breeding dogs should be screened annually; pups can be screened at six to eight weeks of age, before being sold.

RETINAL DYSPLASIA

Retinal dysplasia is an abnormal development of the retina, present at birth. It is presumed to be inherited as an autosomal recessive trait, meaning that both parents must be carriers if a pup is affected. Fortunately, the condition is usually evident on the initial veterinary examination since the problem on the back of the eye can be seen as soon as the eyes are opened at two to three weeks of age. All of the abnormal retinal tissue is typically evident by three to four months of age when the retina is mature. There are no cures although blindness does not occur in all cases. Affected animals, their siblings and parents should not be used for breeding.

SPINAL MUSCULAR ATROPHY

Spinal muscular atrophy is a rare disease but is reported here because it only occurs in Rottweilers. It is evident in young pups as early as four weeks of age. Affected individuals have an enlarged esophagus and so have a tendency to regurgitate their food. By eight weeks of age they have hindlimb weakness, which will eventually progress to include the front legs as well. Typically, the pups do not live more than a few months. Parents and normal siblings of these pups should not be used in breeding programs.

VON WILLEBRAND'S DISEASE

Von Willebrand's disease (vWD) is the most commonly inherited bleeding disorder of dogs. The abnormal gene can be inherited from one or both parents. If both parents pass on the gene, most of the resultant pups fail to thrive and will die. In most cases though, the pup inherits a relative lack of clotting ability, which is quite variable. For instance, one dog may have 15% of the clotting factor, while another might have 60%. The higher the amount, the less likely it will be that the bleeding will be readily evident since spontaneous bleeding is usually only seen when dogs have less than 30% of the normal level of von Willebrand clotting factor. Thus, some dogs don't get diagnosed until they are neutered or spayed and they end up bleeding uncontrollably or they develop pockets of blood (hematomas) at the surgical site. In addition to the inherited form of vWD, this disorder can also be acquired in association with familial hypothyroidism. This form is usually seen in Rottweilers older than five years of age.

Von Willebrand's disease is extremely important in the Rottweiler because the incidence appears to be on the rise. There are tests available to determine the amount of von Willebrand factor in the blood, and they are accurate and reasonably priced.

Rottweilers used for breeding should have normal amounts of von Willebrand factor in their blood and so should all pups that are adopted as household pets. Carriers should not be used for breeding, even if they appear clinically normal. Since hypothyroidism can be linked with von Willebrand's disease, thyroid profiles can also be a useful part of the screening procedure in older Rottweilers.

One symptom of spinal muscular atrophy, which only occurs in Rottweilers, is an enlarged esophagus.

OTHER CONDITIONS COMMONLY SEEN IN THE ROTTWEILER

Amaurosis
Cataracs
Cleft palate
Diabetes mellitus
Distichiasis
Entropion
Iris coloboma
Iris cysts
Macroblepharon
Mandibular distoclusion (overbite)
Mandibular mesioclusion (underbite)
Microphthalmia
Muscular dystrophy
Oligodontia
Parvovirus susceptibility
Persistent pupillary membranes
Refractory superficial corneal ulcers
Retinal degeneration
Retinal detachment
Vitiligo
Wry mouth

INFECTIONS & INFESTATIONS

HOW TO PROTECT YOUR ROTTWEILER FROM PARASITES AND MICROBES

An important part of keeping your Rottweiler healthy is to prevent problems caused by parasites and microbes. Although there are a variety of drugs available that can help limit problems, prevention is always the desired option. Taking the proper precautions leads to less aggrava-

Facing page: A Rottweiler puppy needs a responsible owner who can keep him free of worms, fleas and other ugly invaders. Owner, M. Lazarro.

tion, less itching, and less expense.

FLEAS

Fleas are important and common parasites but not an inevitable part of every pet-owner's reality. If you take the time to understand some of the basics of flea population dynamics, control is both conceivable and practical.

Fleas have four life stages (egg, larva, pupa, adult), and each stage responds to some therapies while being resistant to others. Failing to understand this is the major reason why some people have so much trouble getting the upper hand in the battle to control fleas.

Fleas spend all their time on their host (in this case, your dog) and only leave if physically removed by brushing, bathing or scratching. However, the eggs that are laid on the animal are not sticky and fall to the ground to contaminate the environment. Our goal must be to remove fleas from the animals in the house, from the house itself, and from the immediate outdoor environment. Part of our plan must also involve using different medications to get rid of the different life stages as well as minimizing the use of potentially harmful insecticides that could

be poisonous for pets and family members.

A flea comb is a very handy device for recovering fleas from pets. The best places to comb are the tailhead, groin area, armpits, back and neck region. Fleas collected should be dropped into a container of alcohol, which quickly kills them before they can escape. In addition, all pets should be bathed with a cleansing shampoo (or flea shampoo) to remove fleas and eggs. This has no residual effect, however, and fleas can jump back on immediately after the bath if nothing else is done. Rather than using potent insecticidal dips and sprays, consider products containing the safe pyrethrins, imidacloprid or fipronil and the insect growth regulators (such as methoprene and pyripoxyfen) or insect development inhibitors (IDI) such as lufenuron. These products are not only extremely safe, but the combination is effective against eggs, larvae, and adults. This only leaves the pupal stage to cause continued problems. Insect growth regulators can also be safely given as once-a-month oral preparations. Flea collars are rarely useful, and electronic flea collars are not to be recommended for any dogs.

Vacuuming is a good first step

to cleaning up the household because it picks up about 50% of the flea eggs and it also stimulates flea pupae to emerge as adults, a stage when they are easier to kill with insecticides. The vacuum bag should then be removed and discarded with each treatment. Household treatment can then be initiated with pyrethrins and a combination of either insect growth regulators or sodium polyborate (a borax derivative). The pyrethrins need to be reapplied every two to three weeks but the insect growth regulators last about two to three months, and many companies guarantee sodium polyborate for a full year. Stronger insecticides such as carbamates and organophosphates can be used and will last three to four weeks in the household, but they are potentially toxic and offer no real advantages other than their persistence in the home environment. This is also one of their major disadvantages.

When an insecticide is combined with an insect growth regulator, flea control is most likely to be successful. The insecticide kills the adult fleas and the insect growth regulator affects the eggs and larvae. However, insecticides kill less than 20% of flea cocoons (pupae). Because of this, new fleas may hatch in two to three weeks despite appropriate application of products. This is known as the "pupal window" and is one of the most common causes for ineffective flea control. This is why a safe insecticide should be applied to the home environment two to three weeks after the initial treatment. This catches the newly hatched pupae before they have a chance to lay eggs and perpetuate the flea problem.

If treatment of the outdoor environment is needed, there are several options. Pyripoxyfen, an insect growth regulator, is stable in sunlight and can be used outdoors. Sodium polyborate can be used as well, but it is important that it not be inadvertently eaten by pets. Organophosphates and carbamates are sometimes recommended for outdoor use, and it is not necessary to treat the entire property. Flea control should be directed predominantly at garden margins, porches, dog houses, garages, and other pet lounging areas. Fleas don't do well with direct exposure to sunlight, so generalized lawn treatment is not needed. Finally, microscopic worms (nematodes) are available that can be sprayed onto the lawn with a garden sprayer. The nematodes eat immature flea forms and then biodegrade without harming anything else.

TICKS

Ticks are found world-wide and can cause a variety of problems including blood loss, tick paralysis, Lyme disease, "tick fever," Rocky Mountain Spotted Fever and babesiosis. All are important diseases that need to be prevented whenever possible. This is only possible by limiting the exposure of our pets to ticks.

For those species of tick that dwell indoors, the eggs are laid mostly in cracks and on vertical surfaces in kennels and homes. Most other species are found outside in vegetation, such as grassy meadows, woods, brush, and weeds.

Ticks feed only on blood, but they don't actually bite. They attach to an animal by sticking their harpoon-shaped mouthparts into the animal's skin, and then they suck blood. Some ticks can increase their size 20-50 times as they feed. Favorite places for them to locate are between the toes and in the ears, although they can appear anywhere on the skin surface.

Ticks carry a variety of diseases that could be deadly to your Rottweiler, so be certain to check for them after outdoor adventures.

A good approach to prevent ticks is to remove underbrush and leaf litter and to thin the trees in areas where dogs are allowed. This removes the cover and food sources for small mammals that serve as hosts for ticks. Ticks must have adequate cover that provides high levels of moisture and at the same time provides an opportunity of contact with animals. Keeping the lawn well maintained also makes ticks less likely to drop by and stay.

Because of the potential for ticks to transmit a variety of harmful diseases, dogs should be carefully inspected after walks through wooded areas (where ticks may be found), and careful removal of all ticks can be very important in the prevention of disease. Care should be taken not to squeeze, crush, or puncture the body of the tick, since exposure to body fluids of ticks may lead to spread of any disease carried by that tick to the animal or to the person removing the tick. The tick should be disposed of in a container of alcohol or flushed down the toilet. If the site becomes infected, veterinary attention should be sought immediately. Insecticides and repellents should only be applied to pets following appropriate veterinary advice, since indiscriminate use can be dangerous. Recently, a new tick collar has become available which contains amitraz. This collar not only kills ticks but causes them to retract from the skin within two to three days. This greatly reduces the chances of ticks transmitting a variety of diseases. A spray formulation has also recently been developed and marketed. It might seem that there should be vaccines for all the diseases carried by ticks but only a Lyme disease *(Borrelia burgdorferi)* formulation is currently available.

MANGE

Mange refers to any skin condition caused by mites. The contagious mites include ear mites, scabies mites, Cheyletiella mites and chiggers. Demodectic mange is associated with proliferation of Demodex mites, but they are not considered contagious.

The most common causes of mange in dogs are ear mites, and these are extremely contagious. The best way to avoid ear mites is to buy pups from sources that don't have a problem with ear mite infestation. Otherwise, pups readily acquire them when kept in crowded environments in which other animals might be

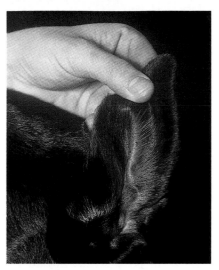

Ear mites are the most common type of mites and are extremely contagious. Keeping your Rottweiler's ears clean is a good first step to preventing mites.

carriers. Treatment is effective if whole body (or systemic) therapy is used, but relapses are common when medication in the ear canal is the only approach. This is because the mites tend to crawl out of the ear canal when medications are instilled. They simply feed elsewhere on the body until it is safe for them to return to the ears.

Scabies mites and Cheyletiella mites are passed on by other dogs that are carrying the mites. They are "social" diseases that can be prevented by avoiding exposure of your dog to others that are infested. Scabies (sarcoptic mange) has the dubious honor of being the most itchy disease to which dogs are susceptible. Chigger mites are present in forested areas, and dogs acquire them by roaming in these areas. All can be effectively diagnosed and treated by your veterinarian should your dog happen to become infested.

HEARTWORM

Heartworm disease is caused by the worm *Dirofilaria immitis* and is spread by mosquitoes. The female heartworms produce microfilariae (baby worms) that circulate in the bloodstream, waiting to by picked up by mosquitoes to pass the infection along. Dogs do not get heartworm by socializing with infected dogs; they only get infected by mosquitoes that carry the infective microfilariae. The adult heartworms grow in the heart and major blood vessels and eventually cause heart failure.

Fortunately, heartworm is easily prevented by safe oral medications that can be administered daily or on a once-a-month basis. The once-a-month preparations also help prevent many of the common intestinal parasites, such as hookworms, roundworms and whipworms.

Prior to giving any preventative medication for heartworm,

an antigen test (an immunologic test that detects heartworms) should be performed by a veterinarian, since it is dangerous to give the medication to dogs that harbor the parasite. Some experts also recommend a microfilarial test, just to be doubly certain. Once the test results show that the dog is free of heartworms, the preventative therapy can be commenced. The length of time the heartworm preventatives must be given depends on the length of the mosquito season. In some parts of the country, dogs are on preventative therapy year round. Heartworm vaccines may soon be available but the preventatives now available are easy to administer and quite safe.

INTESTINAL PARASITES

The most important internal parasites in dogs are roundworms, hookworms, tapeworms and whipworms. Roundworms are the most common. It has been estimated that 13 trillion roundworm eggs are discharged in dog feces every day! Studies have shown that 75% of all pups carry roundworms and start shedding them by three weeks of age. People are infected by exposure to dog feces containing infective roundworm eggs, not by handling pups. Hookworms can cause a disorder known as cutaneous larva migrans in people. In dogs, they are most dangerous to puppies since they latch onto the intestines and suck blood. They can cause anemia and even death when they are present in large numbers. The most common tapeworm is *Dipylidium caninum,* which is spread by fleas. However, another tapeworm *(Echinococcus multilocularis)* can cause fatal disease in people and can be spread to people from dogs. Whipworms live in the lower aspects of the intestines. Dogs get whipworms by consuming infective larvae. However, it may be another three months before they start shedding them in their stool, greatly complicating diagnosis. In other words, dogs can be infected by whipworms, but fecal evaluations are usually negative until the dog starts passing those eggs three months after being infected.

Other parasites, such as coccidia, Cryptosporidium, Giardia and flukes can also cause problems in dogs. The best way to prevent all internal parasite problems is to have pups dewormed according to your veterinarian's recommendations and to have parasite checks done on a regular basis, at least annually.

VIRAL INFECTIONS

Dogs get viral infections such as distemper, hepatitis, parvovirus and rabies by exposure to infected animals. The key to prevention is controlled exposure to other animals and, of course, vaccination. Today's vaccines are extremely effective, and properly vaccinated dogs are at minimal risk for contracting these diseases. However, it is still important to limit exposure to other animals that might be harboring infection. This is particularly important for Rottweil-

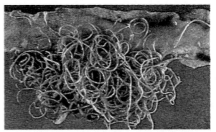

Roundworms affect people as well as dogs, and prevention of these worms is best accomplished by regular veterinary checks ups.

ers because this breed tends to form the weakest protection following vaccination. In fact, we recommend performing tests on parvovirus antibody levels in vaccinated Rottweilers to make sure they produced adequate amounts of antibody. Thus, limiting exposure to carriers is particularly important in this breed.

When selecting a facility for boarding or grooming an animal, make sure they limit their clientele to animals that have documented vaccine histories. This is in everyone's best interest. Similarly, make sure your veterinarian has a quarantine area for infected dogs and that animals aren't admitted for surgery, boarding, grooming or diagnostic testing without up-to-date vaccinations. By controlling exposure and ensuring vaccination, your pet should be safe from these potentially devastating diseases.

It is beyond the scope of this book to settle all the controversies of vaccination, but they are worth mentioning. Should vaccines be combined in a single injection? It's convenient and cheaper to do it this way, but might some vaccine ingredients interfere with others? Some say yes, some say no. Are vaccine schedules designed for convenience or effectiveness? Mostly convenience. Some ingredients may only need to be given every two or more years. Research is incomplete. Should the dose of the vaccine vary with weight, or should a Chihuahua receive the same dose as a Rottweiler? Given their vaccination response, should Rottweilers receive higher vaccine dosages than other dogs?

Good questions, no definitive answers. Finally, should we be using modified-live or inactivated vaccine products? There is no short answer for this debate. Ask your veterinarian and do a lot of reading yourself!

CANINE COUGH

Canine infectious tracheo–bronchitis, also known as canine cough and kennel cough, is a contagious viral/bacterial disease that results in a hacking cough that may persist for many weeks. It is common wherever dogs are kept in close quarters, such as kennels, grooming parlors, dog shows, training classes, and even veterinary clinics. The condition doesn't respond well to most medications but eventually clears spontaneously over a course of many weeks. Pneumonia is a possible but uncommon complication.

Prevention is best achieved by limiting exposure and utilizing vaccination. The fewer opportunities you give your dog to come in contact with others, the less the likelihood of it getting infected. Vaccination is not foolproof because many different viruses can be involved. Parainfluenza virus is included in most vaccines and is one of the more common viruses known to initiate the condition. *Bordetella bronchiseptica* is the bacterium most often associated with tracheobronchitis, and a vaccine is now available that needs to be repeated twice yearly for dogs at risk. This vaccine is squirted into the nostrils to help stop the infection before it gets deeper into the respiratory tract. Make sure the vaccination is given several days (preferably two weeks) before exposure to ensure maximum protection.

Although there are some philosophical questions about effectiveness, cost and frequency of vaccinations, veterinarians never question that your Rottweiler should be inoculated against all infectious diseases.

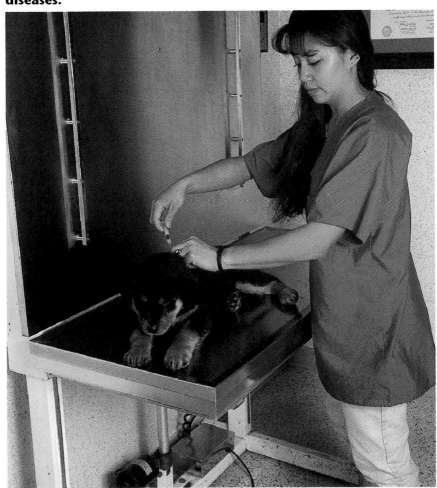

FIRST AID by Judy Iby, RVT

**KNOWING YOUR DOG
IN GOOD HEALTH**

With some experience, you will learn how to give your dog a physical at home, and consequently will learn to recognize many potential problems. If  you can detect a problem early, you can seek timely medical help and thereby decrease your dog's risk of developing a more serious problem.

Every pet owner should be able to take his pet's tem-

Facing page: Don't wait for it to be too late. Learn first aid for your Rottweiler. Owners, Anne and Karen Longo.

Blitz, Liberty and Raach are enjoying their day in the snow. Rottweilers prefer cold weather and are very susceptible to heat-stroke.

perature, pulse, respirations, and check the capillary refill time (CRT). Knowing what is normal will alert the pet owner to what is abnormal, and this can be life saving for the sick pet.

TEMPERATURE

The dog's normal temperature is 100.5 to 102.5 degrees Fahrenheit. Take the temperature rectally for at least one minute. Be sure to shake the thermometer down first, and you may find it helpful to lubricate the end. It is easy to take the temperature with the dog in a standing position. Be sure to hold on to the thermometer so that it isn't expelled or sucked in. A dog could have an elevated temperature if he is excited or if he is overheated; however, a high temperature could indicate a medical emergency. On the other hand, if the temperature is below 100 degrees, this could also indicate an emergency.

CAPILLARY REFILL TIME AND GUM COLOR

It is important to know how your dog's gums look when he is healthy, so you will be able to recognize a difference if he is not feeling well. There are a few breeds, among them the Chow Chow and its relatives, that have black gums and a black tongue.

This is normal for them. In general, a healthy dog will have bright pink gums. Pale gums are an indication of shock or anemia and are an emergency. Likewise, any yellowish tint is an indication of a sick dog. To check capillary refill time (CRT) press your thumb against the dog's gum. The gum will blanch out (turn white) but should refill (return to the normal pink color) in one to two seconds. CRT is very important. If the refill time is slow and your dog is acting poorly, you should call your veterinarian immediately.

HEART RATE, PULSE, AND RESPIRATIONS

Heart rate depends on the breed of the dog and his health. Normal heart rates range from about 50 beats per minute in the larger breeds to 130 beats per minute in the smaller breeds. You can take the heart rate by pressing your fingertips on the dog's chest. Count for either 10 or 15 seconds, and then multiply by either 6 or 4 to obtain the rate per minute. A normal pulse is the same as the heart rate and is taken at the femoral artery located on the insides of both rear legs. Respirations should be observed and depending on the size and breed of the dog should be 10 to 30 per minute. Obviously, illness or excitement could account for abnormal rates.

PREPARING FOR AN EMERGENCY

It is a good idea to prepare for an emergency by making a list and keeping it by the phone. This list should include:

1. Your veterinarian's name, address, phone number, and office hours.
2. Your veterinarian's policy for after-hour care. Does he take his own emergencies or does he refer them to an emergency clinic?
3. The name, address, phone number and hours of the emergency clinic your veterinarian uses.
4. The number of the National Poison Control Center for Animals in Illinois: 1-800-548-2423. It is open 24 hours a day.

In a true emergency, time is of the essence. Some signs of an emergency may be:

1. Pale gums or an abnormal heart rate.
2. Abnormal temperature, lower than 100 degrees or over 104 degrees.
3. Shock or lethargy.
4. Spinal paralysis.

A dog hit by car needs to be checked out and probably should have radiographs of the chest and abdomen to rule out pneumothorax or ruptured bladder.

EMERGENCY MUZZLE

An injured, frightened dog may not even recognize his owner and may be inclined to bite. If your dog should be injured, you may need to muzzle him to protect yourself before you try to handle him. It is a good idea to practice muzzling the calm, healthy dog so you understand the technique. Slip a lead over his head for control. You can tie his mouth shut with something like a two-foot-long bandage or piece of cloth. A necktie, stocking, leash or even a piece of rope will also work.

1. Make a large loop by tying a loose knot in the middle of the bandage or cloth.
2. Hold the ends up, one in each hand.
3. Slip the loop over the dog's muzzle and lower jaw, just behind his nose.
4. Quickly tighten the loop so he can't open his mouth.
5. Tie the ends under his lower jaw.
6. Make a knot there and pull the ends back on each side of his face, under the ears, to the back of his head.

If he should start to vomit, you will need to remove the

muzzle immediately. Otherwise, he could aspirate vomitus into his lungs.

ANTIFREEZE POISONING

Antifreeze in the driveway is a potential killer. Because antifreeze is sweet, dogs will lap it up. The active ingredient in antifreeze is ethylene glycol, which causes irreversible kidney damage. If you witness your pet ingesting antifreeze, you should call your veterinarian immediately. He may recommend that you induce vomiting at once by using hydrogen peroxide, or he may recommend a test to confirm antifreeze ingestion. Treatment is aggressive and must be administered promptly if the dog is to live, but you wouldn't want to subject your dog to unnecessary treatment.

BEE STINGS

A severe reaction to a bee sting (anaphylaxis) can result in difficulty breathing, collapse and even death. A symptom of a bee sting is swelling around the muzzle and face. Bee stings are antihistamine responsive. Over-the-counter antihistamines are available, and you should ask your veterinarian for recommendations on safe antihistamines to use and the doses to administer. You should monitor the dog's gum color and

respirations and watch for a decrease in swelling. If your dog is showing signs of anaphylaxis, your veterinarian may need to give him an injection of corticosteroids. It would be wise to call your veterinarian and confirm treatment.

BLEEDING

Bleeding can occur in many forms, such as a ripped dewclaw, a toenail cut too short, a puncture wound, a severe laceration, etc. If a pressure bandage is needed, it must be released every 15-20 minutes. Be careful of elastic bandages since it is easy to apply them too tightly. Any bandage material should be clean. If no regular bandage is available, a small towel or wash cloth can be used to cover the wound and bind it with a necktie, scarf, or something similar. Styptic powder, or even a soft cake of soap, can be used to stop a bleeding toenail. A ripped dewclaw or toenail may need to be cut back by the veterinarian and possibly treated with antibiotics. Depending on their severity, lacerations and puncture wounds may also need professional treatment. Your first thought should be to clean the wound with peroxide, soap and water, or some other antiseptic cleanser. Don't use alcohol since it deters the healing of the tissue.

BLOAT

Although not generally considered a first aid situation, bloat can occur in a dog rather suddenly. Truly, it is an emergency! Gastric dilatation-volvulus or gastric torsion—the twisting of the stomach to cut off both entry and

BURNS

If your dog gets a chemical burn, call your veterinarian immediately. Rinse any other burns with cold water and if the burn is significant, call your veterinarian. It may be necessary to clip the hair around the burn so it will be easier to keep

Dogs, like people, can become depressed or tired looking when they are sick. Know your Rottweiler in good health so that you can tell when he is sick and needs medical attention.

exit, causing the organ to "bloat," is a disorder primarily found in the larger, more deep-chested breeds. It is life threatening and requires immediate veterinary assistance.

clean. You can cleanse the wound on a daily basis with saline and apply a topical antimicrobial ointment, such as silver sulfadiazine 1 percent cream or gentamicin cream. Burns can be debilitating, especially to an older pet. They can cause pain and shock. It takes about three weeks for the skin to slough after the burn and there is the possibility of permanent hair loss.

CARDIOPULMONARY RESUSCITATION (CPR)
Check to see if your dog has a heart beat, pulse and spontaneous respiration. If his pupils are already dilated and fixed, the prognosis is less favorable. This is an emergency situation that requires two people to administer lifesaving techniques. One person needs to breathe for the dog while the other person tries to establish heart rhythm. Mouth to mouth resuscitation starts with two initial breaths, one to one and a half seconds in duration. After the initial breaths, breathe for the dog once after every five chest compressions. (You do not want to expand the dog's lungs while his chest is being compressed.) You inhale, cover the dog's nose with your mouth, and exhale *gently*. You should see the dog's chest expand. Sometimes, pulling the tongue forward stimulates respiration. You should be ventilating the dog 12-20 times per minute. The person managing the chest compressions should have the dog lying on his right side with one hand on either

side of the dog's chest, directed over the heart between the fourth and fifth ribs (usually this is the point of the flexed elbow). The number of compressions administered depends on the size of the patient. Attempt 80-120 compressions per minute. Check for spontaneous respiration and/ or heart beat. If present, monitor the patient and discontinue resuscitation. If you haven't already done so, call your veterinarian at once and make arrangements to take your pet in for professional treatment.

CHOCOLATE TOXICOSIS
Dogs like chocolate, but chocolate kills dogs. Its two basic chemicals, caffeine and theobromine, overstimulate the dog's nervous system. Ten ounces of milk chocolate can kill a 12-pound dog. Symptoms of poisoning include restlessness, vomiting, increased heart rate, seizure, and coma. Death is possible. If your dog has ingested chocolate, you can give syrup of ipecac at a dosage of one-eighth of a teaspoon per pound to induce vomiting. Two tablespoons of hydrogen peroxide is an alternative treatment.

CHOKING
You need to open the dog's mouth to see if any object is

visible. Try to hold him upside down to see if the object can be dislodged. While you are working on your dog, call your veterinarian, as time may be critical.

DOG BITES

If your dog is bitten, wash the area and determine the severity of the situation. Some bites may need immediate attention, for instance, if it is bleeding profusely or if a lung is punctured. Other bites may be only superficial scrapes. Most dog bite cases need to be seen by the veterinarian, and some may require anti-biotics. It is important that you learn if the offending dog has had a rabies vaccination. This is important for your dog, but also for you, in case you are the victim. Wash the wound and call your doctor for further instructions. You should check on your tetanus vaccination history. Rarely, and I mean rarely, do dogs get tetanus. If the offending dog is a stray, try to confine him for observation. He will need to be confined for ten days. A dog that has bitten a human and is not current on his rabies vaccination cannot receive a

Sparkle, Liberty and Laurel line up for a piece of chocolate birthday cake, but as the owner knows, chocolate's two ingredients, caffeine and theobromine, can be deadly to dogs. Find another treat to give your Rottweiler.

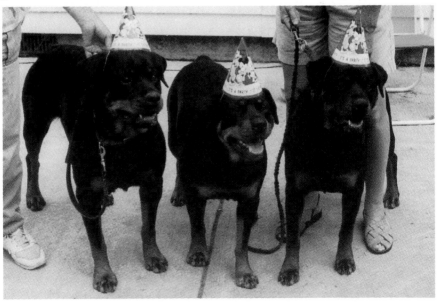

rabies vaccination for ten days. Dog bites should be reported to the Board of Health.

DROWNING

Remove any debris from the dog's mouth and swing the dog, holding him upside down. Stimulate respiration by pulling his tongue forward. Administer CPR if necessary, and call your veterinarian. Don't give up working on the dog. Be sure to wrap him in blankets if he is cold or in shock.

ELECTROCUTION

You may want to look into puppy proofing your house by installing GFCIs (Ground Fault Circuit Interrupters) on your electrical outlets. A GFCI just saved my dog's life. He had pulled an extension cord into his crate and was "teething" on it at seven years of age. The GFCI kept him from being electrocuted. Turn off the current before touching the dog. Resuscitate him by administering CPR and pulling his tongue forward to stimulate respiration. Try mouth-to-mouth breathing if the dog is not breathing. Take him to your veterinarian as soon as possible since electrocution can cause internal problems, such as lung damage, which need medical treatment.

EYES

Red eyes indicate inflammation, and any redness to the upper white part of the eye (sclera) may constitute an emergency. Squinting, cloudiness to the cornea, or loss of vision could indicate severe problems, such as glaucoma, anterior uveitis and episcleritis. Glaucoma is an emergency if you want to save the dog's eye. A prolapsed third eyelid is abnormal and is a symptom of an underlying problem. If something should get in your dog's eye, flush it out with cold water or a saline eye wash. Epiphora and allergic conjunctivitis are annoying and frequently persistent problems. Epiphora (excessive tearing) leaves the area below the eye wet and sometimes stained. The wetness may lead to a bacterial infection. There are numerous causes (allergies, infections, foreign matter, abnormally located eyelashes and adjacent facial hair that rubs against the eyeball, defects or diseases of the tear drainage system, birth defects of the eyelids, etc.) and the treatment is based on the cause. Keeping the hair around the eye cut short and sponging the eye daily will give relief. Many cases are responsive to medical treatment. Allergic conjunctivitis may be a seasonal problem if the dog

While interaction with other dogs is important, supervision is always vital. Should a fight ensue, you must be able to intervene, bearing in mind the safety of your dog and yourself.

has inhalant allergies (e.g., ragweed), or it may be a year 'round problem. The conjunctiva becomes red and swollen and is prone to a bacterial infection associated with mucus accumulation or pus in the eye. Again keeping the hair around the eyes short will give relief. Mild corticosteroid drops or ointment will also give relief. The underlying problem should be investigated.

FISH HOOKS

An imbedded fish hook will probably need to be removed by the veterinarian. More than likely, sedation will be required along with antibiotics. Don't try to remove it yourself. The shank of the hook will need to be cut off in order to push the other end through.

FOREIGN OBJECTS

I can't tell you how many chicken bones my first dog ingested. Fortunately she had a "cast iron stomach" and never suffered the consequences. However, she was always going to the veterinarian for treatment. Not all dogs are so lucky. It is unbelievable what some dogs will take a liking to. I have assisted in surgeries in which all kinds of foreign objects were removed from the stomach and/or intestinal tract. Those objects included socks, pantyhose, stockings, clothing, diapers, sanitary products, plastic, toys, and, last but not least, rawhides. Surgery is costly and not always successful, especially if it is performed too late. If you see or suspect your dog has ingested a foreign object, contact your veterinarian immediately. He may tell you to induce vomiting or he may have you bring your dog to the clinic immediately. Don't induce vomiting without the veterinarian's permission, since the object may cause more damage on the way back up than it would if you allow it to pass through.

HEATSTROKE

Heatstroke is an emergency! The classic signs are rapid, shallow breathing; rapid heartbeat; a temperature above 104 degrees; and subsequent collapse. The dog needs to be cooled as quickly as possible and treated immediately by the veterinarian. If possible, spray him down with cool water and pack ice around his head, neck, and groin. Monitor his temperature and stop the cooling process as soon as his temperature reaches 103 degrees. Nevertheless, you will need to keep monitoring his temperature to be sure it doesn't elevate again. If the temperature continues to drop to below 100 degrees, it could be life threatening. Get professional help immediately. Prevention is more successful than treatment. Those at the greatest risk are brachycephalic (short nosed) breeds, obese dogs, and those that suffer from cardiovascular disease. Dogs are not able to cool off by sweating as people can. Their only way is through panting and radiation of heat from the skin surface. When stressed and exposed to high environmental temperature, high humidity, and poor ventilation, a dog can suffer heatstroke very quickly. Many people do not realize how quickly a car can overheat. Never leave a dog unattended in a car. It is even against the law in some states. Also, a brachycephalic, obese, or infirm dog should never be left unattended outside during inclement weather and should have his activities curtailed. Any dog left outside, by law, must be assured adequate shelter (including shade) and fresh water.

POISONS

Try to locate the source of the poison (the container which lists the ingredients) and call your veterinarian immediately. Be prepared to give the age and weight of your dog, the quantity of poison consumed and the probable time of ingestion. Your veterinarian will want you to

Rottweilers love to swim, so be sure you watch them when they do. A strong current in a river or no way out of the water can lead to trouble.

read off the ingredients. If you can't reach him, you can call a local poison center or the National Poison Control Center for Animals in Illinois, which is open 24 hours a day. Their phone number is 1-800-548-2423. There is a charge for their service, so you may need to have a credit card number available.

Symptoms of poisoning include muscle trembling and weakness, increased salivation, vomiting and loss of bowel control. There are numerous household toxins (over 500,000). A dog can be poisoned by toxins in the garbage. Other poisons include pesticides, pain relievers,

prescription drugs, plants, chocolate, and cleansers. Since I own small dogs I don't have to worry about my dogs jumping up to the kitchen counters, but when I owned a large breed she would clean the counter, eating all the prescription medications.

Your pet can be poisoned by means other than directly ingesting the toxin. Ingesting a rodent that has ingested a rodenticide is one example. It is possible for a dog to have a reaction to the pesticides used by exterminators. If this is suspected you should contact the exterminator about the potential dangers of the pesticides used and their side effects.

Don't give human drugs to your dog unless your veterinarian has given his approval. Some human medications can be deadly to dogs.

POISONOUS PLANTS

Amaryllis (bulb)	Jasmine (berries)
Andromeda	Jerusalem Cherry
Apple Seeds (cyanide)	Jimson Weed
Arrowgrass	Laburnum
Avocado	Larkspur
Azalea	Laurel
Bittersweet	Locoweed
Boxwood	Marigold
Buttercup	Marijuana
Caladium	Mistletoe (berries)
Castor Bean	Monkshood
Cherry Pits	Mushrooms
Chokecherry	Narcissus (bulb)
Climbing Lily	Nightshade
Crown of Thorns	Oleander
Daffodil (bulb)	Peach
Daphne	Philodendron
Delphinium	Poison Ivy
Dieffenbachia	Privet
Dumb Cane	Rhododendron
Elderberry	Rhubarb
Elephant Ear	Snow on the Mountain
English Ivy	Stinging Nettle
Foxglove	Toadstool
Hemlock	Tobacco
Holly	Tulip (bulb)
Hyacinth (bulb)	Walnut
Hydrangea	Wisteria
Iris (bulb)	Yew
Japanese Yew	

This list was published in the American Kennel Club *Gazette*, February, 1995. As the list states these are common poisonous plants, but this list may not be complete. If your dog ingests a poisonous plant, try to identify it and call your veterinarian. Some plants cause more harm than others.

PORCUPINE QUILLS

Removal of quills is best left up to your veterinarian since it can be quite painful. Your unhappy dog would probably appreciate being sedated for the removal of the quills.

SEIZURE (CONVULSION OR FIT)

Many breeds, including mixed breeds, are predisposed to seizures, although a seizure may be secondary to an underlying medical condition. Usually a seizure is not considered an emergency unless it lasts longer than ten minutes. Nevertheless, you should notify your veterinarian. Dogs do not swallow their tongues. Do not handle the dog's mouth since your dog probably cannot control his actions and may inadvertently bite you. The seizure can be mild; for instance, a dog can have a seizure standing up. More frequently the dog will lose consciousness and may urinate and/or defecate. The best thing you can do for your dog is to put him in a safe place or to block off the stairs or areas where he can fall.

SEVERE TRAUMA

See that the dog's head and neck are extended so if the dog is unconscious or in shock, he is able to breathe. If there is any vomitus, you should try to get the head extended down with the body elevated to prevent vomitus from being aspirated. Alert your veterinarian that you are on your way.

SHOCK

Shock is a life threatening condition and requires immediate veterinary care. It can occur after an injury or even after severe fright. Other causes of shock are hemorrhage, fluid loss, sepsis, toxins, adrenal insufficiency, cardiac failure, and anaphylaxis. The symptoms are a rapid weak pulse, shallow breathing, dilated pupils, subnormal temperature, and muscle weakness.

The capillary refill time (CRT) is slow, taking longer than two seconds for normal gum color to return. Keep the dog warm while transporting him to the veterinary clinic. Time is critical for survival.

SKUNKS

Skunk spraying is not necessarily an emergency, although it would be in my house. If the dog's eyes are sprayed, you need to rinse them well with water. One remedy for deskunking the dog is to wash him in tomato juice and follow with a soap and water bath. The newest remedy is bathing the dog in a mixture of one quart of three percent

When outdoors, Rottweilers come in contact with all sorts of vegetation and will sometimes eat harmful plants. Many plants are poisonous, so it's best to know which plants are toxic to dogs.

hydrogen peroxide, quarter cup baking soda, and one teaspoon liquid soap. Rinse well. There are also commercial products available.

SNAKE BITES

It is always a good idea to know what poisonous snakes reside in your area. Rattlesnakes, water moccasins, copperheads, and coral snakes are residents of some areas of the United States. Pack ice around the area that is bitten and call your veterinarian im-

Always remain calm, cool and collected in an emergency situation. Owner, M. Pierce

mediately to alert him that you are on your way. Try to identify the snake or at least be able to describe it (for the use of antivenin). It is possible that he may send you to another clinic that has the proper antivenin.

TOAD POISONING

Bufo toads are quite deadly. You should find out if these nasty little critters are native to your area.

VACCINATION REACTION

Once in a while, a dog may suffer an anaphylactic reaction to a vaccine. Symptoms include swelling around the muzzle, extending to the eyes. Your veterinarian may ask you to return to his office to determine the severity of the reaction. It is possible that your dog may need to stay at the hospital for a few hours during future vaccinations.

RECOMMENDED READING

DR. ACKERMAN'S DOG BOOKS FROM T.F.H.

OWNER'S GUIDE TO DOG HEALTH
TS-214, 432 pages
Over 300 color photographs

Winner of the 1995 Dog Writers Association of America's Best Health Book, this comprehensive title gives accurate, up-to-date information on all the major disorders and conditions found in dogs. Completely illustrated to help owners visualize signs of illness, different states of infection, procedures and treatment, it covers nutrition, skin disorders, disorders of the major body systems (reproductive, digestive, respiratory), eye problems, vaccines and vaccinations, dental health and more.

SKIN & COAT CARE FOR YOUR DOG
TS-249, 224 pages
Over 200 color photographs

Dr. Ackerman, a specialist in the field of dermatology and a Diplomate of the American College of Veterinary Dermatology, joins 14 of the world's most respected dermatologists and other experts to produce an extremely helpful manual on the dog's skin. Coat and skin problems are extremely common in the dog, and owners need to better understand the conditions that affect their dogs' coats. The book details everything from the basics of parasites and mange to grooming techniques, medications, hair loss and more.

DOG BEHAVIOR AND TRAINING
Veterinary Advice for Owners
TS-252, 292 pages
Over 200 color photographs

Joined by co-editors Gary Landsberg, DVM and Wayne Hunthausen, DVM, Dr. Ackerman and about 20 experts in behavioral studies and training set forth a practical guide to the common problems owners experience with their dogs. Since behavioral disorders are the number-one reason for owners to abandon a dog, it is essential for owners to understand how the dog thinks and how to correct him if he misbehaves. The book covers socialization, selection, rewards and punishment, puppy-problem prevention, excitable and disobedient behaviors, sexual behaviors, aggression, children, stress and more.

95

RECOMMENDED READING

ROTTWEILER BOOKS FROM T.F.H.

THE PROFESSIONAL'S BOOK OF ROTTWEILERS
by Anna Katherine Nicholas
TS-147, 446 pages
Over 700 full-color photographs.

THE NEW ROTTWEILER
by Jim Pettengell
TS-202, 287 pages
Over 100 full-color and black/white photos.

THE WORLD OF ROTTWEILERS
by Anna Katherine Nicholas
H-1083, 336 pages
575 full-color photographs.

THE BOOK OF THE ROTTWEILER
by Anna Katherine Nicholas
H-1035, 544 pages
85 full-color photographs.

THE ROTTWEILER
by Richard F. Stratton
PS-820, 256 pages
53 full-color photographs.

THE PROPER CARE OF ROTTWEILERS
by Joan R. Klem & Susan C. Rademacher
TW-142, 256 pages
Over 200 full-color photographs.